THE TRAILS LESS
TRAVELLED

THE TRAILS LESS TRAVELLED
TREKKING THE HIMACHAL HIMALAYAS

AVAY SHUKLA

NIYOGI
BOOKS

Published by

NIYOGI BOOKS

D-78, Okhla Industrial Area, Phase-I
New Delhi-110 020, INDIA
Tel: 91-11-26816301, 49327000
Fax: 91-11-26810483, 26813830
email: niyogibooks@gmail.com
website: www.niyogibooksindia.com

Text © Avay Shukla
Photographs © Avay Shukla (except those credited)
Cover photograph © Srimati Banerjee, Kolkata

Editor: Siddhartha Banerjee
Design: Shashi Bhushan Prasad

ISBN: 978-93-83098-76-7
Publication: 2015

Full-title page: Trek to Pin Parbat Pass; Courtesy: Sanjeeva Pandey

Contents page: Trek in progress in Tirthan valley; Courtesy: Sanjeeva Pandey

Printed at: Niyogi Offset Pvt. Ltd., New Delhi, India

To

Neerja

With deep gratitude and unspoken love

For keeping me company on a far more difficult journey

Contents

Introduction

$\mathcal{H}$imachal offers the nature-traveller and trekker the entire gamut of the Himalayas—from the Shivalik foothills to the mid-Himalayas, to the trans-Himalayas, to the Greater Himalayas in the northernmost districts of Lahaul-Spiti, Chamba, and Kinnaur. In keeping with this variety of terrain, it has the most variegated trekking portfolio for the adventurous-minded: cold deserts, high mountains, alpine pastures, dense forests, and windblown passes. Embedded in this God-sculpted terrain are the most beautiful lakes and water bodies imaginable, majestic glaciers that dare Man to approach them, and rivers and streams gushing with the sheer joy of life as they flow down to the distant plains to sustain hundreds of millions of lives. Adding to this richness is the abundance of wildlife at high altitudes—Himachal has 12 per cent of its geographical area (almost 7,000 sq. km) under the Protected Area Network comprising 2 national parks and 32 wildlife sanctuaries. Almost all of the high-altitude trekking routes pass through these protected areas and offer the traveller the unique opportunity of sighting the rare wildlife of these temperate forests and alpine pastures, including the highly endangered snow leopard, Spiti wolf, musk deer, and western tragopan pheasant. There are also the black bear, brown bear, ghoral, bharal, common leopard, and monal pheasant.

The state has a very strong and distinctive cultural DNA, which becomes immediately evident to persons who travel off the beaten track and into the interiors where the linkage to tradition is still valued.

Ice bridge on way to Bhim Dwar

Page 8: Campsite at Parkatchi Thatch

Himachal is known as "Dev Bhoomi" or the land of gods, and every little village and valley has its own *devta* or deity, imbuing each trek with its own mythological aura and adding a unique facet to one's travels in the more remote areas. Every local *devta* has his list of "dos" and "don'ts" and these have to be scrupulously respected. The Pandavas of *Mahabharata* fame are believed to have spent some period of their exile in the mountains of Himachal; the interiors are replete with stories (and landmarks and features) of their travels.

The ubiquitous tentacles of development, however, are taking a massive toll on the state's natural assets and it is almost certain that most of the landscapes (and the lives, culture, and myths they contain) described in these pages would be altered beyond recognition within the next 10 years, or would simply cease to exist. The rapacious quest for ever-higher GDP figures and rent-seeking by successive governments are ensuring that an increasing number of cement plants, hydel projects, road construction, and unregulated proliferation of the internal combustion engine have crept into the most interior and pristine areas of the state and are now eating into its innards like some unstoppable cancer. Dense forests are being devastated (more than 100 sq. km of forestland and 7,00,000 trees have been sacrificed for the purpose in the last 20 years), rivers and streams are being recklessly dammed, diverted and dried up, valleys are being filled up with the debris of road and other construction activities. The beautiful, once untouched natural landscape of the state is witnessing the ever-enlarging footprint of modern man. There is, therefore, a certain poignancy in the actual writing of the pages that follow for what they describe may not exist in a few years—the gods would be remembered by no one, the caveman would have been relocated to a new concrete building, and the tragopan would have vanished into the mists of time.

TREKS IN
SHIMLA
DISTRICT

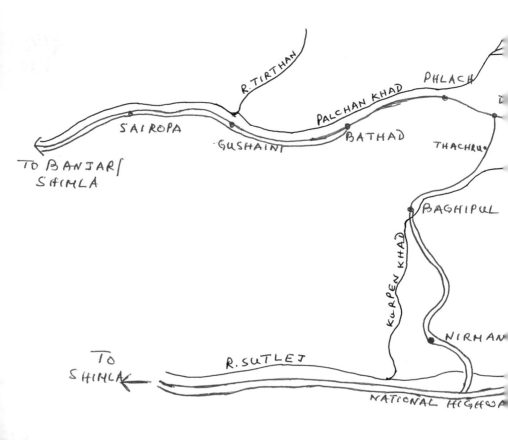

R. TIRTHAN

PHLACH

PALCHAN KHAD

SAIROPA

GUSHAINI

BATHAD

THACHRU

TO BANJAR/
SHIMLA

BAGHIPUL

KURPEN KHAD

NIRMAN

TO
SHIMLA

R. SUTLEJ

NATIONAL HIGHWA

MAP NOT TO SCALE

MOTORABLE ROAD

TREK ROUTE

VILLAGE / CAMP SITE

△ MOUNTAIN PEAK

RIVER / STREAM

 LAKE

N

Srikhand Mahadev

SRIKHAND
MAHADEV

NAIN
SAROVAR

HIM
DWAR

TO
RAMPUR/
KALPA

Srikhand Mahadev—there is a majestic resonance to these words, almost a spiritual chant. And well there might be, for this peak is considered to be the abode of the god Shiva, soaring a majestic 5,227 metres and perhaps the most difficult pilgrimage in Himachal Pradesh. Situated precisely at the border of Shimla and Kullu districts, and further overlooking Kinnaur district, the mountain attracted about 25,000 visitors in the year 2003, mainly *yatris* comprising of local people from the three aforementioned districts; but it is gaining popularity in the state of Punjab too. Not all make it to the peak though; we were told that about 30 per cent of the pilgrims give up on the last day's ascent to the peak, so difficult is the last stretch. The season of worship extends from July to end-September and is flagged off with a "Chhari Yatra" by saints and holy men sometime in the second or third week of July, usually coinciding with Shravan Ashtami. Earlier the pilgrims had to fend for themselves, but in recent years prominent local citizens of the Nirmand area of Kullu have formed a Srikhand Mahadev Seva Samiti, which assists the devotees by providing tented accommodation and setting up langars (eateries) along the route—all without any charge.

There are three routes to Srikhand Mahadev. The most favoured track, and the one followed by 90 per cent of visitors due to its being relatively easier than the other two, is the one from Baghipul, which is the last point on a motorable road. Baghipul is a one-horse village on the Kurpen stream; to get to it one has to drive from Shimla to about 10 km before the sub-divisional town of Rampur Bushehar, cross the Sutlej to its right bank, proceed to Nirmand (a sub-divisional headquarter of Kullu district), and continue another 17 km to Baghipul. The rest of the journey from here is on foot—about 35 km, usually done in two days. The second and most difficult route is from Jeori (the roadhead). It is located about 180 km from Shimla on the main Hindustan–Tibet road to Kinnaur district. At Jeori, one again crosses the mighty Sutlej and proceeds up the Ghanvi Khad on foot, across a place called Phancha, meeting up with the track from Baghipul about a thousand feet below the peak. Although much shorter than the first route (it takes one-and-a-half days to reach the peak) it is a much more difficult option, risky at places where one has to cross a number of glaciers and negotiate sheer precipices. It is best left to the locals to opt for this route. There is also a third, relatively unknown route, which would lie somewhere between the other two in the degree of difficulty. This too intersects the main Baghipul route about 20 km before the peak, on the second day. Since we were more interested in trekking rather than the religious aspect of the journey, and therefore not too imbued with the *yatri* spirit, we decided to take this third route in August 2003.

The journey starts from a place called Sai Ropa; to get there one has to cross the river Beas at Aut, about 25 km before Kullu on the main Mandi–Kullu highway, and turn right. Proceeding downstream along the left bank of the Beas for a couple of kilometres, one crosses the river Sainj and enters the Tirthan River valley a couple of miles further on. The contrast between the two streams is immediately obvious—while the waters of the Tirthan are a pristine blue-green, those of the Sainj are a pale muddy brown, a dubious contribution of the construction activities at the Parbati Hydel project going on at full swing in the latter valley. Following the Tirthan upstream on its left bank for about eight kilometres one quickly reaches Sai Ropa, a small village at an altitude of 4,000 feet, which is also the headquarters of a forest range office. It also contains a well-appointed complex of the Biodiversity Conservation Society of the Great Himalayan National Park (GHNP), housing an information centre, conference rooms, and a small rest house. This acts as the point of origin for treks and excursions into the GHNP, the boundaries of which are located just a few kilometres away, and also forms the ideal starting point for the trek to Srikhand Mahadev.

After spending the night at Sai Ropa we left the next morning at 8 am—the motorable road continues for another 15 km past a little hamlet called Gushaini, where the Tirthan meets the Palchan Khad, and then along this khad to Bathad where the road ends. (Between Sai Ropa and Bathad we counted the signboards of five micro-hydel projects slated to come up in this area. These small projects, all between 500 kW and 2 MW, are far more preferable than the huge Parbati-type projects because they require very little civil works and are therefore much more eco-friendly). Bathad has the peculiar distinction of a solid concrete bridge spanning the Palchan Khad, but with no approach roads to it from either side! We were informed that the bridge had been standing in such splendid isolation for the last three years because the Public Works Department (PWD) had run out of money to acquire the private lands through which the approach roads were to be constructed! In all likelihood, by the time funds are forthcoming, the bridge would have been washed away in some flash flood and everything would have reverted to its original state of innocence—except, of course, the contractors and engineers concerned, who would have moved considerably farther on the road to economic prosperity.

Shouldering our rucksacks we began the walk—initially level till Galiar village along the Palchan Khad, the track quickly became a steep ascent as it started to climb out of the khad. Thirty minutes or so later we crested the top at a village called Machhiar (2,600 metres). This is a considerably large village, divided into three distinct clusters with acres of cultivated fields on all sides. There was also strong evidence that people here grow poppy and "bhang". Straight ahead and across the khad lay the Bashleo Pass. Machhiar contains a fairly ancient temple, which, to our horror, we found painted a garish blue, red, and yellow. It looked more like the gate to a marriage pandal than an old temple. On enquiring, we were informed that the paint job had been carried out recently on the instructions of the local sub-divisional magistrate (SDM)—an enthusiastic but totally misguided effort that blasphemes tradition and culture.

From Machhiar it is 18 km to the campsite for the first day's night-halt—a place called Phlach. It is almost a forced march from here on, thanks to the lack of a suitable camping site on this entire stretch. This goes against the usual trekking logic that the first day's hike should not be strenuous and should be intended more to loosen and "break in" the muscles. For those who are particular about this precautionary measure, it would be better to camp at Machhiar itself for the first day. We, however, pressed on, leaving Machhiar at about 1:00 pm after having lunch at the local school. The track follows the roaring waters of Palchan Khad, climbing steadily through a thick forest of oak and hill bamboo which gradually gives way to birch and spruce. The undergrowth is extremely thick, coming up to one's waist, and since it had rained in the morning, we were soaked to our armpits in no time at all. So thick is the vegetation here that the trail is hardly visible and one has to be careful in placing one's foot. It is an exasperating trek because one is constantly climbing and descending, following the contours of the khad. Quite often, so steep-walled is the khad, the trail simply disappears and one has to hop from rock to boulder with the foaming waters lapping at one's feet and soaking the boots. At some point we entered the limits of Tirthan Wildlife Sanctuary; there are no markers to indicate its boundaries. After about 10 km of this gruelling progress, the track crosses over to the left bank of the stream over a rickety wooden bridge and, thankfully, starts climbing out of the khad. The trees begin to thin out, giving way to the *bhojpatra* and then to juniper and dwarf rhododendron, the undergrowth being replaced by verdant grasslands. Within a couple of kilometres of crossing the

stream the treeline completely disappears, revealing the contours of a
beautiful vale running in an East–West direction, the stream flowing in
the same alignment (we were entering the valley from its western end).
The valley is closed from three sides: on its north and south flanks
steep walls rise a thousand feet, plateauing out to beautiful pastures
at the top; its eastern end is blocked by a 12,000-foot-high rampart,
from which originates the Palchan. The elevation of the valley floor
itself would be no more than 9,500 or 10,000 feet—not high enough
for the treeline to completely disappear. However, here the treeline
had actually disappeared at about 9,000 feet, perhaps because the
enclosed valley creates its own microclimate, trapping mist and clouds
and bringing down the temperature. In any case, at about 7:00 pm we
reached Phlach, our campsite for the night. Phlach consists of nothing
more than a huge overhanging rock under which one can camp even if
one has no tents, which is what the local shepherds do. There is plenty

*Campsite at
Phlach*

of level ground for pitching tents, and sparkling clean water can be obtained from the stream nearby.

Day two should begin early as one has to cover about 20 km to reach Bhim Dwar, base camp for the next day's climb to Srikhand Mahadev. One cannot stop for the night before Bhim Dwar because: (a) there are no suitable places, and (b) the last day's trek is difficult enough from Bhim Dwar; from any greater distance, it would be an ordeal. We had an early breakfast of hot tea and aloo parathas and left at 7:00 am, climbing gradually to the saddle on the massif on the eastern end of the valley. This climb is incredibly enjoyable—a 2,000-foot ascent through the valley floor covered with a thick carpet of grass and alpine flowers, followed by gently rounded slopes rising to high pastures demurely veiled by softly moving clouds that part occasionally to reveal the distant peaks of Shimla. En route to the top we passed a Gaddi settlement of about 500 fat sheep, three Gaddis, and two imposing sheep dogs, also known locally as Gaddis. It is a dog breed indigenous to these parts of the Himalayas, about the size of a big Labrador or Retriever but much heavier in the neck and head. Its head and jaws are its most distinctive traits, and their sheer size leaves no room for doubt that these dogs are bred to take on the leopard and the brown bear, also inhabitants of these regions and a constant threat to the flocks. This courageous breed, I am told, has finally been given its long overdue recognition by being categorised as a distinct breed by the Kennel Club of India—it is now officially known as the Himalayan Mastiff. It is typically a languid and docile breed, but essentially half wild and almost impossible to domesticate. I should know for I tried to raise one! Some years ago I acquired a beautiful black Gaddi pup from the area beyond Rohtang Pass, characterised by a huge head and simply enormous paws. I kept Rex in my house in Shimla for four months, and realised during that time how hard it is to train or domesticate an animal that is 75 per cent wild. Gaddis by instinct don't sleep at night since that is when they are supposed to be on guard—Rex would be padding up and down the house the entire night, keeping everyone awake. His massive jaws constantly needed something to work on, and thus, within a very short period of time, the wood panelling on the walls of the house had been chewed off and a beginning made on the floorboards! Rex's genes must have constantly reminded him of the limitless alpine pastures that his forefathers roamed because we could never get him to accept a collar or a leash. He would break free from them in no time at all with his enormous strength and just run away, sometimes for a couple of days. But even at that young age his homing instincts, or sense of smell or direction, were so strong that he invariably came back. He inherently had no sense or concept of fear, making it impossible to train him or to discipline him. Finally, I accepted the inevitable—that his wild spirit craved for the freedom to be found in nature alone and that he could not be anything but true to his blood or genes, shaped by the high peaks and pastures of the Himalayas as it were. He was not meant to be brought up in a flat in Shimla. So I gifted Rex to Raman, a friend who owns a large orchard five hours away from Shimla, and both are reported to be quite happy with the arrangement (although the monkeys who earlier used to infest Raman's orchard may have a different take on it!).

The Gaddi encampment is known as Chatri; a thousand feet above is the saddle on the high ridgeline, known as Chatri Top and also called Pattu Burji (3,950 metres). It is at this point that we saw our first Brahma Kamal—a huge lotus-shaped flower—growing among the rocks; one of the rarest high altitude flowers about which I shall relate more later. Summiting Pattu Burji and looking eastward towards the peaks of Shimla district, the contrast was immense. While the approach from the western side was gentle and grassy, the ridge fell away abruptly on the eastern side revealing sheer rocky precipices engulfed in foaming clouds and mist, making one wonder whether in fact there was any trail down that side. There was a faint, barely discernible goat track clinging to the sheer rock faces, which gradually gave way to scree and moraine and then to scrub and grass. Thick mist hung all around and it made sense for us to stick together lest anyone got lost. After about 1,500 feet of descent we hit the track coming from the south—the conventional route from Baghipul taken by all the *yatris*—at a point known as Dunga Thua. The

12-km stretch from here to Bhim Dwar is extremely tiring despite the fact that this track is usually in better shape. There are at least a dozen deep nullahs or gullies cutting across it from the left, and each one has to be negotiated by climbing down about a hundred feet into the nullah and then climbing out again with no net gain in altitude to show for all this effort! Some of these nullah crossings are quite tricky—they are either rushing torrents that have to be crossed by hopping from one rock to the other, hoping that there is no slippery moss growing on any of them, or are spanned by huge snow bridges with water gushing under them. One has to walk over the snow bridges, of course, praying like crazy that they don't collapse under one's weight!

After a tiring journey we reached Bhim Dwar at about 7:00 pm. Located at a height of 3,600 metres, Bhim Dwar is not a particularly attractive place and looks quite forlorn. The valley here is about half

Campsite at Bhim Dwar

a kilometre wide with a small stream flowing down its middle and *Waterfalls at* *Bhim Dwar* high mountains on all sides. The valley itself is aligned in a North–South direction—we entered from the south and to the north soars the Srikhand peak, though not visible from here. The meadow at Bhim Dwar is quite spread out and offers very good camping options; in fact, the Srikhand Mahadev Seva Samiti has even prepared some tenting sites here. This is also prime camping area for the Gaddis and their flocks, though by September they start moving down. The surrounding mountain slopes are lush green and at least three beautiful waterfalls are visible, cascading into the valley to form the stream that flows down its middle. There reverberates a continuous roar from the combined might of the waterfalls; we went to sleep that night in our tents shrouded in the mist and rumble of the waters flowing down from Shiva's abode.

The third day's trek is extremely demanding—one has to cover eight kilometres to the Srikhand peak, climbing 1,600 metres, and return to Bhim Dwar as camping in the freezing temperatures above is not a sensible option. An additional sobering factor is the weather since it can and does change suddenly at these heights. Therefore, the peak must

be attained by noon and the return journey started as soon as possible thereafter. We commenced our journey by 6:00 am, even before the rising sun had hit the towering peaks surrounding Bhim Dwar. The first four kilometres are a gentle ascent through soft, thickly padded pastures. Crossing a couple of deep nullahs, the path winds its way up in a serpentine manner to a tabletop meadow about 250 metres high, which blocks the northern end of the Bhim Dwar valley. From its crest one gets the first, distant, mist-shrouded view of the Srikhand peak, on one's left, in a roughly north-north-west direction, behind a high ridgeline. It looks deceptively close but is still hours of hard climbing away.

From the meadow the track follows a watercourse in a straight line; ascending steadily, the soft earth gives way to moraine and scree, and the climb gets harder. A few more Brahma Kamal blossoms came into view, the first we had seen after Pattu Burji. Another hour or so later we arrived at Nain Sarovar—a fairly big glacial lake surrounded by high, barren, glaciated slopes. And all around, sprouting profusely from the rocks, were hundreds of Brahma Kamal blossoms, creating an amazing floral landscape in a rocky wasteland. This area is known, quite mellifluously, as Parvati ka Bagicha, and thereby hangs one of the most poignant myths that this *dev bhoomi* abounds with. Legend has it that while Shiva was ensconced in deep meditation on the Srikhand peak, the goddess Parvati became passionately enamoured of him. She was so desperate to have him as her consort that she meditated, undertook *tapasya* at this spot for 18,000 years! Even the forces of nature empathised with her and thousands of Brahma Kamal flowers sprouted up all around—these are supposed to be Parvati's favourite flowers—and hence the name given to this place: Parvati ka Bagicha, or the garden of Parvati. At one point in her prolonged meditation Parvati got so disheartened that she started weeping and a solitary teardrop fell to the ground. This is believed to have formed a lake in the shape of an eye and is thus called Nain Sarovar. It is myths like this which anthropomorphise these stark and imposing mountains, imbue them with a timeless wonder and grandeur, people them with the living ghosts of our ancestors and a myriad gods, and make us return to

them again and again, notwithstanding the obvious travails and dangers attached to them. Himachal, especially, is blessed with such mountain mythology where every peak and valley has its pantheon of gods and goddesses. Without the faith that these myths inspire and the meaning that this faith generates, life in these harsh and occasionally cruel climes would be virtually unbearable. And though the itinerant trekker might not believe in these myths and legends in a rational sort of way, he still respects and values them, and marvels at this coming together of the forces of man, religion, and nature.

Prayer flags with Nain Sarovar in the background

Nain Sarovar is gradually filling up with silt as the glaciers that feed it slowly retreat and the run-off brings with it rocky detritus from the surrounding barren slopes. This problem is not peculiar to Nain Sarovar and applies to almost all high mountain lakes in this state. It poses a fundamental dilemma for nature lovers—should we intervene to save these incomparable lakes, or should we back off and let nature take its own course? On one hand, the processes of nature are dynamic, shaping and reshaping the geographical features of these regions over the aeons, creating, destroying, and recreating. One lake may fill up over time while another may be created some place else. Any human intervention in these natural rhythms may well have a disastrous effect on the entire ecosystem of these very fragile mountains and disturb the balance of natural forces created over thousands of years. (A prime example of this is the beautiful Khajjiar Lake above Dalhousie in Chamba district. Every single act of intervention by the government to stop it from shrinking has made it even smaller, and it is now on the verge of being silted over completely). On the other hand, the languid pace of nature has undoubtedly been accelerated by the actions of man and the changes now taking place in the environment may be too rapid for nature to absorb. Consequently, the entire rhythm of the natural forces may have gone awry. Destruction may not be followed any more by recreation and the changes we are now witnessing may well be irreversible. So, should we take steps to preserve these jewels in the lap of the mountains? I am afraid there are no easy answers.

Nain Sarovar is, however, now being subjected to another, more directly related manmade problem about which we can certainly do something. Underwear! It is almost mandatory for pilgrims to take a dip in the holy waters of this lake before proceeding to the peak. And over the last couple of years this ritual has been accompanied by a peculiar practice—the bathers leave their underwear behind in the lake! We were told that the lake bed is now littered with these undergarments, polluting its pristine purity. This trend was first noticed in the even holier Manimahesh Lake in Chamba district; the district administration there has to spend a lot of time and effort in cleaning up the lake every year since the number of people visiting Manimahesh is much larger. It appears that this insidious practice has now arrived at Nain Sarovar. The Seva Samiti is planning to launch a cleanup operation soon, which is certainly welcome, but there is also a need to educate the *yatris* to the ill effects of this pernicious practice. (Perhaps the authorities should simply put up barriers around the lakes and ensure that everyone takes off their underwear before taking a dip.) Just as the director of the Great Himalayan National Park (who was part of our trekking team) was doing for the conservation of the flora of the area. He had brought with him a dozen signboards advising visitors not to pluck the medicinal plants or flowers that grow here since these are seriously endangered. These boards were put up at prominent places along the trail and are bound to have a healthy and constructive effect.

We had a quick lunch at Nain Sarovar and girded our loins for the final 1,300-metre climb to the peak. Towering above the lake is a steep scree-covered slope about 300 metres high and its very sight is daunting, especially after three aloo parathas! It is easier to climb such slopes than descend on them because one can get some traction on the loose soil and scree when climbing, but is unable to obtain a firm grip and is constantly slipping and sliding on the way down. We negotiated this slope in surprisingly good time—about 25 minutes—and even saw a snow partridge en route. From the crest of the ridge one can also see Kartike in the north-east, about five kilometres as the crow flies. Kartike (named after a son of Shiva) is the sister peak of Srikhand. It is conical in shape and much more difficult to scale, even though its height is less than that of Srikhand; perhaps the reason why it has not acquired the same religious status as the latter. This is also the point at which the track from Kinnaur/Jeori meets the main track via Phancha village. But when we crested the top our collective hearts missed many beats—there was no sight of the peak! Instead, what we saw was row upon row of boulder-strewn ridges, each higher than the last one. There was no trail at all, only massive boulders. We had to jump and claw our way up from one rock to another; a single misjudgement or slip could only end in a fracture or a sprain. This is the most difficult portion of the trek as it stretches over three kilometres and also involves an ascent of about a thousand metres. It is an unrelenting climb, and we were told that many *yatris* pull out at this point and go back. We pressed on for about an hour and came to a site known as Bhim ki Bahi, about 200 metres below the peak. The place gets its name from the strange and intriguing rocks here: strewn about are dozens of huge, rectangular-shaped tablets with peculiar, hieroglyphic-type markings on them. These rock tablets look completely out of place among the other, rounded boulders that form this landscape—they appear to have been shaped by some deliberate, conscious force. Also, the markings on them appear to be some primitive form of writing, certainly not the result of erosion or weathering. Legend has it that these are the registers (*bahi*) of accounts and events maintained by Bhim when the Pandavas were roaming in these lands during their *banwas* or exile. Unlikely? I never scoff at something I cannot rationally explain. So far, no one has been able to give a rational explanation for these *bahis*, nor is it likely in the foreseeable future considering that we still have to decipher the writings and inscriptions found at Mohenjo-Daro and Harappa.

About two hours after leaving Nain Sarovar we came to a glacier about hundred metres wide, and on its far side stood the huge monolithic rock that forms the peak of Srikhand Mahadev. The monolith is about 20 metres high, black and grim, and does not appear to be an integral part of the mountain; it appears to

The Srikhand Mahadev peak
Courtesy: Sanjeeva Pandey

have been placed or planted there. The whole mountaintop is fractured into separate, loose pieces with only this rock standing as a single entity. This is the Shiva Linga which people worship. Some hardy locals even climb to the top of the feature and plant flags there. Next to the Shiva Linga is a smaller rock that is worshipped as the consort of Shiva, Parvati. One has to approach the two rocks barefoot which, for us, limited the time we could spend on prayers due to the freezing cold. The time was about two in the afternoon and the weather had taken a turn for the worse—clouds and mist had blown in from the east. Thus, after spending just half an hour at the top, we began our return journey. We reached Bhim Dwar at about 7:00 pm, totally exhausted but still impressed at the raw grandeur and unexplained mysteries of the mountain we had left behind.

On day four we commenced our return journey, this time via the main track to Baghipul, happy that the toughest part of the trek was behind us. But we were to discover that some fairly arduous stuff still lay ahead. The first 12 km to Dunga Thua was common to the route we had taken on the way up. Just after this intersection point is Kalighati ka Sar, which consists of a small temple, and a pond behind a check dam constructed by the forest department. It's a good place to take a break for just beyond it is the steep, 1,500-foot climb to the top of a ridge very appropriately called Danda Dhar (3,500 metres). There is again a small temple on its crest, situated amidst beautiful pastures, and the view from there is breathtaking. From the top it's a gentle descent of about three kilometres to Thachru—a clearing in a thick oak forest where the Seva Samiti has built some sheds, laid a water pipeline, and organises free langar for the *yatris*. This watershed is drained by the Kurpen stream, which is visible far below as a tiny ribbon of white, and our hearts sank when we were informed that we had to descend to the stream and cross over to the far bank. The descent is about 2,000 feet and quite steep, but it is through dense forests of kharsu oak, spruce, birch, and *Taxus baccata*. The last one is a fairly rare species whose leaves and bark have established anti-cancer properties, and the tree is consequently in great demand by the pharmaceutical companies. Local Gaddis (shepherds) boil the bark of this tree along with their tea or milk and claim that it keeps them free from various ailments.

The climb down to the Kurpen is extremely tiring, more so because it comes at a time when one is psychologically conditioned to think that the difficult part is over. It takes about two hours and one finally sees the welcome sight of the bridge that spans the Kurpen Khad. Crossing over to the right bank, one follows the stream downstream for about four kilometres of fairly level walking, almost along the riverbed itself. Forty-five minutes later one arrives at the hamlet of Samatan, consisting of all of 10 houses and one enchanting little forest inspection bungalow with electricity, running water, and even an electric geyser! It is such a pleasant sight after the longest day of trekking so far—about 30 km. Adjacent to the rest house is a small temple and a complex consisting of sheds, dormitories, and toilets built by the Seva Samiti for the convenience of *yatris*. We spent that evening in delicious relaxation before a huge bon-fire. Our porters and some of the local people even put up a *nati* show for us (the local Himachali folk dance) in which we also took a few tired steps!

The trek was practically over and so we took it easy the next day, getting up late and breakfasting almost at leisure. But the sun can get really hot here and it is advisable not to tarry too long, for about eight kilometres still remain to be covered on foot till the roadhead at Baghipul. It's a pleasant walk to Baghipul through lush cultivated fields and orchards, once again along the Kurpen but now above it. It was apple season and we saw entire families busy in stacking trays and cartons, ready to pack the fruit for transportation to the market. The government is building a motorable road from Baghipul to Singh Dwar village on this route and we could see that work was going on at full swing. It will probably take a couple of years but when the road is complete, trekkers and *yatris* would be able to go all the way to Samatan by road.

We reached Baghipul at 11:00 am after about one and a half hour's walk. From here one can catch a bus or take a taxi to Nirmand, Rampur, or Shimla. The first thing we did was go to a tea shop, order hot tea and toasts, and scan through the newspapers of the last five days. We read that some politician from Haryana had been stabbed on Mall Road in Shimla, the Opposition was still trying to pull down Mayawati in Uttar Pradesh, and the Himachal Pradesh government had ordered its fourth round of transfers in as many months. In other words, nothing had changed in this sordid, materialistic world of ours; Srikhand Mahadev, with its Nain Sarovar, Brahma Kamals, and beautiful myths now seemed to exist in an entirely different universe. We were glad that we were given a glimpse of that world too.

2003

TREKS IN
KINNAUR
DISTRICT

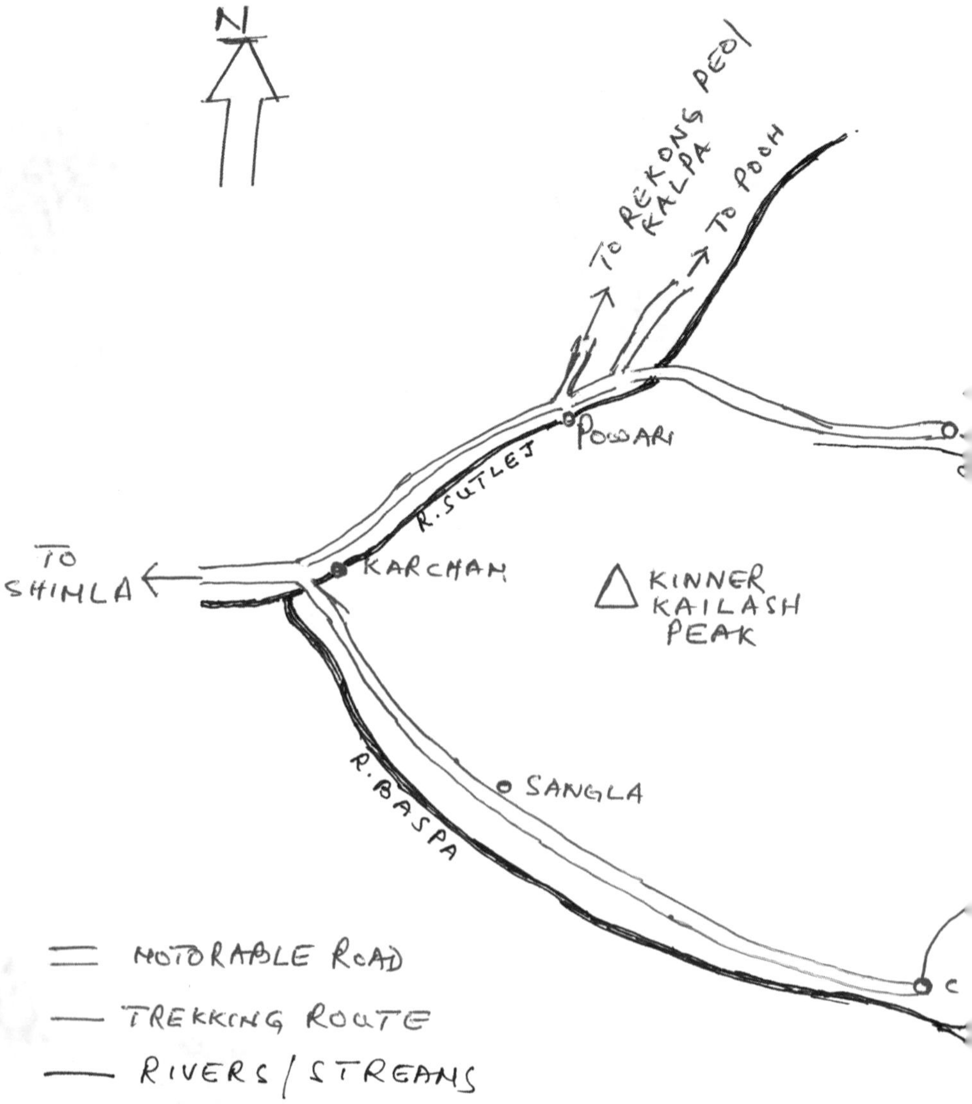

N

To REKONG PEO/
KALPA

To POOH

POWARI

R. SUTLEJ

TO
SHIMLA

KARCHAM

△ KINNER
KAILASH
PEAK

R. BASPA

○ SANGLA

═══ MOTORABLE ROAD

─── TREKKING ROUTE

─── RIVERS/STREAMS

\\ PASS

○ VILLAGE/CAMP SITE

MAP NOT TO SCALE

Raldang Kora
PARIKRAMA OF THE
KINNER KAILASH

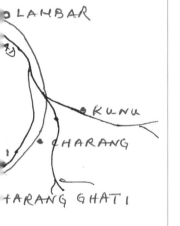

*T*he Kinner Kailash massif lies in a west to north-east alignment in the Kinnaur district of Himachal Pradesh, which borders Tibet. It soars to a height of 20,000 feet, and is held sacred by the local tribals as it is believed to be the abode of a veritable pantheon of Hindu gods. It also abounds with mythical tales of the Pandavas who are believed to have spent some time in these mountains. Raldang—home of the gods—is the generic name given to the many peaks that cap the massif. Kora means a circuit of the entire range or a *parikrama*. A *parikrama* of the Kinner Kailash is generally held to be of spiritual importance and equivalent in status to the Kailash-Mansarovar yatra.

The *parikrama* originally used to start from Karcham, about 20 km below and before (as one comes from Shimla along the Sutlej valley) Reckong Peo, the headquarters of Kinnaur district. The route it took thereafter led to Powari, Akpa, Thangi, Lambar, Charang, Lalanti, over the Charang Ghati Pass and down to Chitkul, Sangla, and finally back to Karcham. The circumambulation is done with the mountain range on one's right-hand side, as is customary in Hindu religious rites. The entire circuit covers a distance of approximately 220 km and was originally traversed on foot, which would take upto seven or eight days. The journey takes the traveller from an altitude of about 7,000 feet (Karcham) to almost 18,000 feet (the Charang Ghati or Pass, or Charang La, as referred by the locals). Nowadays however, with the expansion of the road and transport network, the *parikrama* usually begins at Thangi and terminates at Chitkul, reducing the distance to be covered on foot by as much as a hundred kilometres. It can now be conveniently completed in four days, with night halts at Lambar (10,000 feet), Charang (11,500 feet), Lalanti (14,000 feet), and Chitkul (11,500 feet). The most suitable time of the year for the circuit is the July–September period, the only available window between melting of the previous winter's snow and onset of the coming winter. About 400 persons undertake the *parikrama* every year including tourists and even foreign nationals, now that the area is no longer a restricted one from the defence point of view. Surprisingly, there are absolutely no facilities provided by the state government. Therefore, it is important that the intending trekker or pilgrim is self-sufficient in all matters, starting from tents to food. The few villagers along the route are, of course, hospitable to a fault as only the Kinnauras can be, but there is only so much that they can do with their limited resources.

We undertook the journey in the last week of August; our party consisted of about 15 persons and half a dozen donkeys. A few words about these donkeys would not be out of place here since they are such humble but fascinating creatures. Quite different from their better-known cousins-in-burden the mule, the Kinnaur donkey is a master of his environment. Small in size, in a terrain where every living organism has to be small to survive, it stands barely three feet high at the shoulder and can typically carry about 40 kg only. But they are extremely hardy, can live off the sparse vegetation available at these altitudes, and can negotiate the narrowest and steepest of mountain paths and tracks. They can maintain a steady pace of six to eight kilometres per hour, almost twice the speed of the average trekker. This makes them ideal backpack animals. They are also highly skilled at their job—they know their routes, where to give way to other traffic on the narrower paths, and even the traditional halting points on trekking expeditions! They never complain and need very little supervision, making them indispensable and invaluable companions on a trek.

The first day's trek is merely an introduction to the rigours that come later. We left Thangi at about 2:00 pm and trekked gently upwards along the Charang Khad, following the course of a fairly large stream that was to be our constant companion for two days—sometimes calm and placid, sometimes gurgling and tinkling like a playful child, sometimes roaring and foaming in anger at being restricted by the towering rocky walls, but always beautiful and enchanting in its various moods. The pines gradually gave way to the more hardy spruce and juniper. Wild apricots grew in abundance along our route, to be later harvested by the local villagers who have worked out a family sharing system. Apricots fetch a very good price in the markets of Delhi and Punjab, and the oil from their seeds (chulli oil) can be used for cooking, massages, and even as hair oil. The state government had started construction of a road from Thangi but since it had progressed only about 500 metres in the last five years, the local people were not particularly enthused by the idea. (This road has now progressed up to Lambar, though it is fit only for four-wheel drives).

We reached our first camping point at 5:00 pm after having covered a distance of about 10 km. The place is called Lambar, a tiny hamlet on the banks of the stream, consisting of precisely four houses and a population of 27. Even this small number, however, was a divided lot. The people of Kinnaur have hearts as warm as their environment is cold; add to this the special composition of our party and the reason for this division in paradise became clear at once. Our group included the divisional commissioner of Shimla, the superintendent of police, and the additional deputy commissioner of Kinnaur. Such a high-powered group had never been to this area in the past and was not likely to in the future either. Each of the four families of Lambar, therefore, wanted to host dinner for us, and since no agreement could be arrived on this, the village had formed two amicable camps and both were expecting us for dinner that night. We managed to arrive at a kind of compromise that required us to wine at one house and dine at the other.

The "wine" of Kinnaur is probably the biggest hazard the unwary trekker is likely to face. Known by the generic name *angoori* or the far more accurate *ghanti*, it is distilled from the juice of grapes, apricot, or even the humble barley. The first distillate is called *rashi* and the second, *moori*. The drink is very fruity and radiates warmth throughout the body from the very first drop. Having absolutely no pretensions at subtlety, it does not creep up on you—the first sip itself delivers the kick of a hundred mules! And the *moori* is such a pure and concentrated potion that in any other place it would be classified as an explosive! Fortunately for us what was on offer that night was the milder *rashi,* and so we could make it to our tents without falling into the stream or the next valley.

It is always advisable to complete as much of the day's trek as possible by noon as after that the sun's rays become too strong in this rarefied atmosphere. Thus, we broke camp at 5:00 am the next morning and resumed our ascent along the Charang Khad. This second day's trek was more difficult because now, there was no defined path. We walked along the stream bed, or rather hopped from one boulder to another, which is an extremely tedious and tiring process leaving one with no opportunity to observe the landscape. The Charang stream is snow-fed and so we were surprised to notice that its waters were a turbid grey-black. It was only later that we realised why—most of the terrain through which it flows consists of very loose soil strata almost entirely devoid of any vegetation, and any rain in its catchment washes this soil into the stream, giving it this peculiar colour. Fortunately, this is an arid zone in the rain shadow of the mountains, so this does not happen very often. In fact, by the evening of the second day, the waters had cleared up considerably.

About 15 km and four hours from Lambar, after we had crossed over to the left bank of the stream, we were delighted to be met by a small group of villagers who were carrying parathas and pots of tea in the most exotic and biggest thermos flasks I have ever seen! These wonderfully friendly people were from Kunnu, a small village on the right bank of the stream—it was visible from our rendezvous point, about two kilometres away across the stream. They had heard that we were passing that way and had forded the stream, which at this point is about two to three feet deep but very fast-flowing and achingly cold, just so that they could give us some refreshments! The *up-pradhan* (deputy of the village headman) was there with his very pretty young wife, and I have never had tea that tasted better. After this short break the doughty *up-pradhan* again forded the stream to escort his wife to the other side, and re-forded it because he insisted on accompanying us to Charang!

At about this point the Charang Khad widens out and simultaneously forks out into two valleys, each with their own streams—Charang is situated in the valley on the left and Kunnu on the right (as one looks

Up-pradhan of Kunnu village and his wife crossing the Charang stream

upstream). The Tibetan border is quite close to this point and can be reached in two days' strenuous trekking. This gives the area a strategic importance and is the reason why this area was out of bounds for non permit holders till a few years ago. A modest but unofficial cross-border trade still exists and the flasks we saw were perhaps proof of that. But there must be easier ways of making money. Maybe the Federation of Indian Chambers of Commerce and Industry (FICCI) could institute a special award for these people for it will never see a bolder or finer spirit of entrepreneurship.

Charang consists of about 40 houses and is dominated by a Buddhist monastery or *gompa,* run by a group of Buddhist nuns or *chomos.* Our party included three scholars of ancient architecture led by Deborah Klimburg-Salter, a professor from the Institute of Tibetan and Buddhist Studies at the University of Vienna. At the time we undertook this trek, Deborah had already done some valuable work on the more famous Tabo and Nako monasteries, and had come up to further study the Charang *gompa* for she had a feeling that this was at least as old as Tabo and of eleventh-century vintage. If her more detailed examination confirms this that would put Charang on the world map! The monastery has an interesting collection of ancient Tibetan weapons, another reminder of the close historical and cultural links that existed between this area and Tibet before outsiders decided to play politics with the centuries. Local legend has it that many centuries ago the village was attacked by Tibetans who came on foot from across the mighty passes. When all appeared lost the local deity intervened—she caused the valley to reverberate with the sound of galloping horses, and the Tibetans, thinking that a large force was coming to the rescue of the village, fled leaving behind all their weapons. These were the ones so carefully preserved in the monastery.

The village has one tiny two-roomed staging hut of the irrigation department, set amidst ample grounds and apple trees, and this is where we pitched our tents. At about 11,500 feet it was colder than Lambar but still bearable. Like Kunnu, Charang has electricity supplied by diesel generators stationed there by the state electricity board. We learnt that the board had drawn up a scheme to construct a transmission line from Thangi to bring power to the three villages in the valley. The whole idea is totally impracticable and will only be a waste of public money. Construction of such a line over about 40 km of this rugged terrain would be prohibitively expensive, and maintaining it even more so given that it can snow as much as five to six feet here. There is so much water in the valley; what the govt should do is to put up a small 25 kW micro-hydel project on any of these streams at a central point, specifically dedicated to supplying power to these three villages only. This would be less expensive, quick, easier to maintain, and much more reliable. It would transform the lives of the people who certainly deserve much more from a govt that claims to have electrified all the villages in the state. (I now learn that a couple of micro-hydel projects have indeed been sanctioned by the government for this area.)

Our third day began as usual—a cup of tea and we were off at 7:00 am. We had to first climb out of the valley: a steep ascent of about a thousand feet, which was quite pleasant because it was exclusively over soft pasture land, the grass and flowers still wet with the overnight dew. Once we crested the top of the ridge, however, the picnic was over. In front of us was a steep descent over rocks and boulders, down a thousand feet into a narrow valley at the bottom of which flows a small, crystal clear stream that empties into the main Charang Khad further down. We trekked up along this stream, climbing steadily for about 10 km. Snow-capped peaks now appeared in front of us—one of them, still unnamed, had been scaled by Chris Bonington many years ago. The valley gradually opened out, the stream dividing into many tongues with each warbling its own language. At about two in the afternoon, after covering about 20 km, we reached Lalanti. At this point we had to cross over to the left bank of the stream but without the benefit of any bridge! The glaciers from which the stream was born were barely 10 km away and within 30 seconds of being in the knee-high waters, I had lost all sensation in my legs. The sheer force of the current took one's breath away; it also took away a pair of boots and a walking stick!

Campsite at Lalanti

Lalanti consists of camping grounds, a shepherds' hut, and a couple hundred sheep. The people of Thangi have traditional grazing rights here and camp here with their sheep from May to the beginning of September. They were now in the process of packing up for their migration down south as the mercury had been steadily dipping in the last few days. We were now at 14,000 feet. We had seen absolutely no wildlife in the three days that we had been trekking, even though we were told that the area does have some ibexes and snow leopards. In fact, the *fual* (shepherd) informed us that a snow leopard had killed five of his sheep at that very spot just three days ago. (Whether he was telling the truth or just wanted to extract some compensation from the divisional commissioner, I don't know, but we did kind of stay close together for the rest of the night). The *fual* added to our wildlife lore by informing us that the snow leopard is a wanton killer who does not kill only for food but for the sheer heck of it. Not being very big, it cannot break an animal's neck like a tiger or a leopard; it kills by grabbing the throat and choking the victim to death. That is the reason why all the guard dogs accompanying the flock wear collars with wicked spikes on them. The spikes prevent the snow leopard from seizing them in a killing grip.

The cold at this height was quite severe and thus, after imbibing some of the statutory *ghanti* and hot mutton soup (courtesy the *fual*, who was well stocked with mutton after the snow leopard's visit), we took to our tents and were lulled to sleep by the oddly comforting sound of the donkeys grazing around us. We had pitched our tents away from the stream, not only because Malpa was still fresh in our minds but for another interesting reason. Apparently, the water level of glacial streams starts to rise late in the afternoons and evenings as the melt-off increases the longer the sun has been at work on the ice and snow. By the evenings these streams are at their highest levels and hence our precaution. We had been warned that the fourth and final day's trek would be a real killer, involving at least 12 hours of trekking, and so we left Lalanti at six in the morning. The donkeys could no longer accompany us as the track was now too precipitous and we bid farewell to these humble beasts of burden. A thick fog enveloped us as we started out, guided only by the stone cairns erected along the track by pilgrims who had gone before. We had reason to be grateful for these cairns; without their guidance we would have been hopelessly lost. Visibility was less than 10 feet and since we were a large group, we kept in touch by whistling—a peculiar mountain sound that can cover amazing distances, and is both a question and intimation. We continued to follow the stream for about three hours and then turned right for the final stage of the ascent to the base of Charang Ghati Pass. The terrain now consisted entirely of rocks and boulders, brought down by rains and the incessant erosion of timeless years. Encircling us were towering snow-capped peaks in a horseshoe formation, and we were headed for the centre of the horseshoe where the pass was located.

Looking up at the snow-clad Charang Ghati Pass

It was all a grind now and we had no time or inclination to pause and admire the rugged vistas around us. The vegetation now consisted of huge outcrops of moss that were at least an inch thick at some places, shrubs, and carpets of tiny flowers of the most amazing hues between boulders. They reminded me of a little verse by Wordsworth that I had read in school a lifetime ago:

> A violet by a mossy stone
> Half hidden from the eye!
> Fair as a star, when only one
> Is shining in the sky.

This entire area leading up to the pass is supposed to fall under the dominion of Chitkul Devi, the presiding deity of Chitkul temple situated on the other side of the pass, and she has decreed that no one must pluck any flowers on their way to the pass. This very conservationist edict is observed quite faithfully and the land is better for it. We were now at 16,000 feet and some of us were beginning to feel it. We naturally attributed the incremental shortness of breath to the lower oxygen content in the air but the locals have another explanation for it. According to them the various herbs and bushes give off an aroma which causes breathlessness and headaches. The antidote they suggested for this is to place a piece of garlic in the mouth while climbing. I had no need to try this out but I personally have no reason to doubt either the diagnosis or the cure; these people live in complete harmony with their environment and understand every nuance of it. Once or twice I saw a dark, oily patch under some of the bigger boulders, which could have been wet moss or could have been the mystical *shilajit*—a thick, viscous unguent that is almost pure calcium, exuded by the rocks. So strong are its properties that it is considered almost a miracle cure for joining broken bones. (I can personally vouch for its amazing efficacy. In 2007, I had broken my spine at two places and also fractured four ribs in a freak accident. One of my Kinnaura friends sent me *shilajit*, which I took religiously. I was back on my feet in six weeks and trekking and playing golf again in six months! The doctors had told me I would never be able to do either ever again). *Shilajit* sells for as much as a thousand rupees for 10 grams, but 99 per cent of what is available in the market is spurious. The real stuff is very difficult to come by—it is only available at altitudes above 15,000 feet, and the finding of it is totally random and fortuitous as no one knows how, why, where, and when it is produced. Only the shepherds and *fuals*, who wander this forbidding terrain for six months in the year, sometimes stumble upon a tiny deposit by sheer chance, and they usually don't sell it, keeping it for the use of their own families and friends. I, of course, didn't come to know all this till much later and thus, never investigated the dark patches I saw; in all probability, even if I had known, I doubt I would have stopped for fear of being left behind in this totally intimidating terrain!

We reached the base of the pass at about 11:00 am. It is not a particularly pretty spot, the boulders giving it quite the devastated appearance, but it is somewhat saved by the fact that the glacier which feeds the stream we had been following for the last two days ended here and we could literally see the birth of a river system. Just dipping my hands into these fresh waters gave me a feeling of closeness to nature that is difficult to put into words; one has to experience it to understand what I mean. Directly ahead of us was the pass and our hearts sank as we gazed up at it. It was a sheer wall of moraine and earth, 500 metres high and at an angle of almost 90 degrees. There was no defined path to the top, which left us wondering how we would ever get there.

By now we had been joined by another dozen or so persons—a group of five Kinnaura belles who would keep our spirits high by singing all the way to the top, seven sturdy young policemen, and two septuagenarian shepherds. We began our ascent at 1:30 pm and first had to negotiate a rockfall about 25 metres high and 200 metres wide. Beyond this, one has to take a transverse, zigzag route all the way to the top. The steep slope consisted entirely of loose earth and shale, and given the sharp gradient, for every two steps forward we slid back one. There were occasional patches of snow through which we somehow slithered our way up. The climb was back-breaking and sometimes risky because of the treacherous surface underfoot. We reached the pass at 3:30 pm—it had taken us almost two hours to negotiate these 500 metres.

The view from the pass was stupendous: on the northern side (from where we had come) were range upon range of snow-capped peaks and glaciers from which flowed white ribbons of streams and rivulets. The southern Chitkul side, however, was completely shrouded by a cloak of dense clouds through which emerged peaks of the range that separated Sangla valley from the tehsil of Dodra Kwar. The pass itself was just a rocky saddle, barely 10 feet wide and about 50 feet long. It was festooned with scores of white flags planted there by

pilgrims. Travellers traditionally inscribe their names on them and have them blessed in the monastery at Charang. It was extremely windy at this height, and cold. We tarried just long enough to perform the ritual puja, plant our flags, and get our breath back, after which we began our descent.

The descent to Chitkul is awesome, for lack of a better term. It is not just that one has to descend about 7,000 feet over a 10-km distance, after already having trekked 20 km and climbed 4,000 feet that day. It is the monotony of the bleak terrain that gives no respite to the eyes or the aching leg muscles. The descent is in three distinct stages with each stage marking a descent of about 2,000 feet. The first, from the pass itself, is the most precipitous, and involves sliding and skidding down a mixture of loose earth, pebbles, and scree. This ends in a massive

Valley of the Baspa River on Chitkul side of the pass. Beyond the river is the Rupen Pass leading to Dodra Kwar

rockfall area, comparatively level and about two kilometres long. It is easy to lose one's way over this terrain since there is no discernible track, and therefore, one has to look out for the stone cairns and markers along the way. The only way to traverse this stretch is to jump from rock to rock, a process that is not only extremely tiring but also fraught with risk for the rocks can be slippery and unstable, and one's concentration can also waver. The second stage of the descent begins where the rockfall ends—this is a steep incline of loose earth and one has to jink one's way down like a sidewinder. This is a treacherous stretch because there is nothing to stop one if he or she were to slip. It is therefore advisable to negotiate this stage in a group. The saving grace, however, is that midway through this stretch one catches the first glimpse of Sangla valley, far below in the distance no doubt but green and verdant, a total contrast to the rocky wasteland one finds oneself in at this point. A sliver of the Baspa River can now be seen at the bottom of the valley, as can the ribbon that is the road which connects Chitkul and Sangla. They are all still a long way off but at least the end is in sight! The third stage is much easier—though still quite steep, the footing is much better, the stark rocks giving way to welcome shrubs and bushes. On the far side of the valley, beyond the Baspa, the unbelievably beautiful pastures of Sangla become visible, huge swathes of green meadow surrounded by thick clusters of forests. There are some lovely trekking routes in that area too.

Finally, at about 6:00 pm, we reached Chitkul through a pleasant grove of dwarf willows, flourishing no doubt because of the edict of the Chitkul Devi. Chitkul is the last village in Sangla valley, without a doubt the most picturesque valley in the state. Beyond it lie only the massive empty pastures known as Rani Kanda, patrolled by the Indo-Tibetan Border Police. Special permits are required from the office of the deputy commissioner of Kinnaur for proceeding beyond Chitkul even today. (When I made this trek in 2000, Chitkul was a tiny village with just one government rest house. It has grown considerably since then, thanks to tourism, and on a good day in the summer season, can receive as many as a couple of busloads of visitors, largely Bengalis. It now boasts of a few homestays also!) As per custom we went straight to the temple of the Devi to seek her blessings and to thank her for safe passage through her mountain dominions. Traditionally, the Devi can ask a worshipper for any offering and the latter has no option but to oblige. Conversely, she can also bestow any gift on any follower if it so pleases her. Interestingly enough, we were informed that just the previous week three Gorkha labourers who had come to the temple were rewarded by the Devi with 5,000 rupees each! We had no such luck. After making our offerings we boarded vehicles for the hour-long drive to the state electricity board rest house at Sangla, completing the *parikrama* on which we had started out five days ago.

2000

TREKS IN
KULLU
DISTRICT

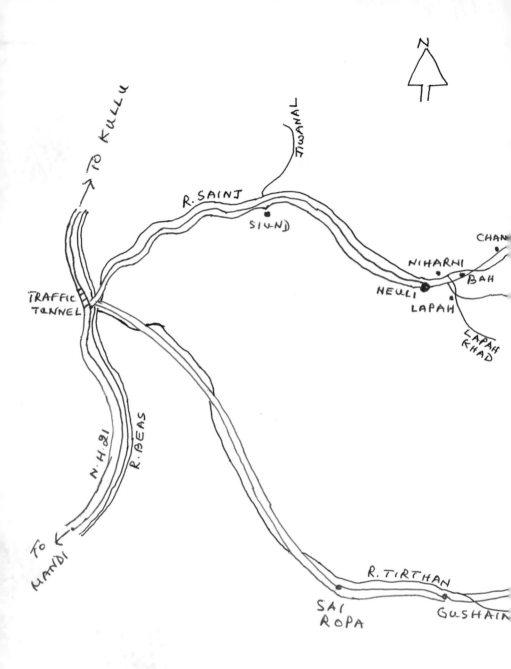

N

TO KULLU

JIWANAL

R. SAINJ

SIUND

CHAN

NIHARNI

BAH

NEULI

LAPAH

TRAFFIC
TUNNEL

LAPAH
KHAD

N.H.21

R. BEAS

TO
MANDI

R. TIRTHAN

SAI
ROPA

GUSHAIN

MAP NOT TO SCALE

═ MOTORABLE ROAD
─ TREKKING ROUTE
• VILLAGE / CAMPING SITE
△ SADDLE
─ RIVER / STREAM.

Dhela Thatch
THE HEART OF THE
GREAT HIMALAYAN NATIONAL PARK

*T*here is a special kind of exhilaration when trekking in winter conditions, even at mid-altitude locales. One can go up to 8,000 feet or even higher, but one should avoid the high alpine pastures and mountain passes where the weather can deteriorate abruptly and snowfall can cut off all exit routes. The Great Himalayan National Park (GHNP) in Kullu offers some great trekking opportunities in winter.

The GHNP trek starts at Neuli (1,200 metres), a tiny hamlet 30 km up the Sainj valley after crossing the river Beas at Aut. Neuli is on the western boundary of the GHNP and is located in its ecozone area, a buffer between the park and the villages surrounding it. One proceeds in a north-east direction along the Sainj River, past the even tinier hamlets of Niharani, Baha, Chenga, and Denga, through dense forests of alder, tosh, and bamboo which gradually give way to conifers, oak, and deodar as the elevation increases. We managed to spot three typical but rare birds of the Himalayan region: the brown dipper, the Himalayan blue whistling thrush, and the plumbeous water redstart, which makes its living in the most difficult way imaginable—diving into the furious currents, almost disappearing under the freezing waters for as much as 20 seconds at a time, only to catch small insects! It incidentally gets its name from its stark red bottom! Five kilometres from Denga one enters the Sainj Wildlife Sanctuary. The first day's trek of 21 km ends at Shakti (2,400 metres), a village of about 20 houses. There is a trekkers' camp here with running water, toilets, and a kitchen, but no electricity. Park officials suspect Shakti to be the hub of poaching and illegal extraction of rare medicinal plants and mushrooms, particularly of Gucchi (Morel, which sells for as much as Rs 20,000 a kilo in Delhi) from the sanctuary and national park. From here one can continue eastwards, up the Sainj for another day, to the hamlet of Marour. The more interesting trek, however, is to Dhela Thatch, south of Shakti.

The next day we had a leisurely breakfast and left camp at 8:00 am. Almost immediately we were met by the local schoolteacher (Shakti has one government primary school), known simply as Shastriji, who requested us to visit his school and meet the children. We had time to spare so we agreed. He took us on a track which soon branched out of the village track and instead climbed about 100 metres above it (away from the river), ending in a large cave overlooking the valley. Shastriji stopped and gestured at the cave: "Welcome to the Shakti Primary School, sirs," he announced with some glee! We could not believe our ears—who had ever heard of a school in a cave in this twenty-first century? But Shastriji was not joking. Apparently, in accordance with a government policy that a primary school would be opened wherever a certain number of school-going children were present, the education department had some years ago sanctioned a school for Shakti and posted a teacher (Shastriji) here. It completely forgot the need of a building for the school! Poor Shastriji, his entreaties got lost somewhere in the long chain of command. He had also tried to get one of the villagers to offer a room in his house but people here do not trust the government, so this attempt too met with no success. Finally, being made of sterner stuff than either his department or the villagers had suspected, he located this cave and established his school here! We took a round of the cave and found that he had actually arranged it quite artfully. It was a large cave, about 25 feet deep and 10 feet wide. Shastriji had divided it into halves by hanging a bed sheet across the middle, effectively creating two rooms. The front room, which overlooked the village, was the school, and the rear one was his personal quarters. The cave provided a splendid view of the Sainj valley and the forested escarpment on the other side leading up to Dhela Thatch. The school had been functioning in this manner for the last three years. If ever a public servant deserved a medal it had to be Shastriji. We had a cup of tea with him and left him with assurances that we would definitely do something about this sorry state of affairs when we returned to Shimla. (This story has a happy ending. I took up the matter with the minister of education who was genuinely surprised by this startling news, especially when he learnt that it was in his own constituency! He immediately sanctioned a building for the school and when I revisited Shakti a couple of years later I was happy to see a spanking new school building there. Shastriji, of course, was no longer there—someone had heard his pleas and transferred him to an easier station).

Dhela is 12 km from Shakti—after crossing over to the left bank of the Sainj over a quaint wooden bridge, one enters GHNP proper. (The bridge I first crossed over in 2002 was washed away in floods a few years later; the forest department has now replaced it with a sturdier wooden structure). GHNP is a unique expanse of 754.40 sq. km of pristine Himalayan vegetation and forests, home to some of the most endangered wildlife in the world, including the snow leopard and the western tragopan, and a veritable repository of hundreds of valuable medicinal plants. Ruthlessly exploited in the past, they are all making a slow but steady comeback since the declaration of this area as a national park some 25 years ago. One climbs steadily, first through abandoned fields and orchards (acquired by the government for the park) and then through dense forests of broad-leafed species such as walnut, jamun, horse chestnut, and maple. These gradually change to fir and deodar, which in turn give way to brown oak and spruce. There are signs of invisible wildlife all around—clearings where the brown bears have dug up the ground to get at their favourite shoots and roots, the bark of an occasional tree with long scratch marks where the bear has sharpened

its claws or scratched its back, walnut shells with neat holes drilled through the middle where the kernel has been extracted surgically by the nutcracker, the sudden flapping of invisible wings when a startled monal pheasant takes flight. Fascinating in any season, this walk through the heart of the GHNP is almost a spiritual experience in the winter when the entire forest is carpeted with snow, the massive trees stand like white wraiths, and a total primordial silence envelops the world, forcing one to look inwards, to reassess everything one has experienced, learnt, or believed in till that moment. Our footfalls made no sound at all, smothered as they were by the deep snow; the only sounds that disturbed the stillness of the forest were the soft "plops" of lumps of snow falling from the trees. After about six hours one reaches Dhela Thatch (3,737 metres), a huge clearing located just below the ridgeline that separates the Sainj and Tirthan valleys. The view from here is spectacular: to the north is the massive Khandadar massif rising more than 16,000 feet, to the north-west is the even higher Pin Parbat range, to the south-east the Tirthan ridge, and beyond that the bleak ranges on which is located the holy peak of Srikhand Mahadev. Fortunately, there is no habitation at Dhela, just one trekker cabin and plenty of fine open space to pitch a dozen tents; a stream meanders nearby and there is plenty of fallen timber for campfires. Dhela is located about 100 metres below the ridgeline; half a kilometre above the campsite, on the ridgeline itself, is a huge cairn of stones dedicated to a local deity. Referred to as *jognis*,

FACING PAGE:
A waterfall in the Great Himalayan National Park

Trekking party with the Khandadar range in the background

such cairns can be seen on all the passes and ridges where shepherds and locals travel—they are man's homage to the mighty elements that rule here and whose moods can mean the difference between life and death. They also serve a more practical purpose—visible on the skyline from a long way off, they serve as useful route-markers, especially in bad weather or when one is lost. Below the *jogni* is a vast thicket of juniper and dwarf rhododendron where the monal and the occasional tragopan come to feed at sunset. The *jogni* is an ideal hide for spotting these birds. The western tragopan (*Tragopan melanocephalus*) is the most famous denizen of this park and the primary reason for the park's fame—the GHNP is one of only two remaining habitats of this most elusive of pheasants (the other being Daranghati Sanctuary in Shimla district). It is locally known as the *juju rana* or "king of birds". Legend has it that after God had created all manner of birds and animals, he was not satisfied and still yearned to create a masterpiece. He summoned all the birds of the universe and asked them to contribute the most beautiful colour of their being. Putting all their colours together, he then created the *juju rana*— truly one of the most exotically coloured and strikingly beautiful birds in the world. Winter is an ideal time to spot this shy creature at Dhela as, with the advent of snow in the higher reaches, it migrates to lower altitudes. Its habitat is not the canopy or the trees but the undergrowth of bushes and hill bamboo, and Dhela offers a perfect combination of all of them. However, descending to lower altitudes in the winters makes this rare bird vulnerable to poaching as it comes within reach of the scattered villages. Habitat disturbance due to development projects and poaching have made the tragopan the most endangered of all pheasants. There is no official census of its population but most forest officials agree that there cannot be more than a few hundred in the two areas of the state that comprise its habitat—GHNP itself and the Daranghati Wildlife Sanctuary in upper Shimla district. Concerned at its dwindling numbers, the state forest department has started an artificial breeding programme for the bird at a place called Sarahan in Shimla district, though with limited success. It has been successful in getting them to breed in captivity (a couple of dozen chicks have been born there) but the most difficult part still lies ahead: controlled release of the birds in the wild. The programme is being guided by the Royal Pheasant Association of the United Kingdom which, apparently, is the world leader when it comes to breeding pheasants. They breed as many as six million birds in captivity each year, release them in the wild, and then shoot them! Pheasant shooting in that country is almost a national sport, next only to fox hunting. Ghoral or the Himalayan mountain goat can also be sighted on the cliffs jutting out from the ridge, especially in the early morning when they come out to graze in the warm rays of the rising sun.

One should spend at least two days at this idyllic place, soaking in the sun and the view, spotting wildlife, listening to the serenades and sonatas of the birds at dawn and dusk. There are two options before the trekker when proceeding from here. The first involves staying on in the Sainj valley or catchment area and returning via a steep descent of 1,700 metres to the south-west into the Lapah Khad, a tributary of the Sainj. The Lapah stream, a fairly substantial body of water, originates somewhere south of Dhela below the ridgeline and meets the left bank of the Sainj above Neuli, between Niharani and Baha. The route into Lapah gorge starts from the *jogni* on the ridge above Dhela in a west-north-west direction and quickly descends almost 2,000 metres to the stream. It makes long traverses through an overgrown forest of oak and pine which, for some strange reason, is infested with flies and mosquitoes! This is a feature I have never encountered in any other high-altitude forest and even the forest officials accompanying us could not account for it. It is, however, reason enough not to tarry in the forest: it is not a pleasant walk for, in addition to these insects, there is absolutely no view since this is almost a gorge and the trapped air is still and humid. It takes about three hours to reach the Lapah stream at the bottom. Across this stream are the twin villages of Lapah-Dhara (2,400 metres) consisting of about 30 houses. There is a two-roomed forest hut where one can stay. Lapah stream marks the western boundary of the GHNP. The residents of these twin villages are much better off than their unfortunate counterparts in Shakti and Marour as they are outside the protected area (though within the park's ecozone) and thus have fewer restrictions on their activities. They are also home to a troupe of folk singers consisting of young school-going boys and girls. This *"kala jathha"* (literally, artistic group) is sponsored and funded by the management of GHNP to spread the message of conservation to all the neighbouring settlements. It is an innovative and brilliant idea conceived by Sanjeeva Pandey, director of the park. The populations surrounding the GHNP, on whose cooperation the very survival of the park depends, are generally illiterate and cannot absorb abstract notions of conservation, protection of biodiversity, and natural heritage as couched in the lexicon and arguments of the present. The *kala jathha* instead transmutes these messages and weaves them into local folklore, religious practices, mythology, and the simple rhythms of nature—something that these villagers have lived with for hundreds of years and comprehend instantly. The *jathha* does this through music, pantomime, and play-acting. We were able to witness the effectiveness of their strategy ourselves since a show was held the very evening we were there! Men, women, and children from all the surrounding villages came to attend the show, and were captivated by the performance of

Dhela Thatch with the trekkers' hut in the foreground

Sanjeeva climbing out of the Sainj valley

these young boys and girls. I can only wish Sanjeeva and his young volunteers greater strength. One can take it easy the next day since the route is only about three hours over a gently descending track along the Sainj back to Neuli.

The second trekking option from Dhela is to crossover to the Tirthan River valley in the south, a spectacular but much more difficult trek—I would definitely recommend this option. It takes three days and begins again from the *jogni*; one goes along the ridgeline in a southerly direction for about four kilometres. The view here is awe-inspiring: one is blinded by the sight of dozens—yes, dozens—of 4,000- and 5,000-metre peaks, set in an arc spanning from the north-east to the south and encompassing the very core of the park. It is all ice, glaciers, and untouched nature in that direction for dozens of miles with no human populations, the way Nature meant it to be. The ridgeline through which one walks is actually a verdant alpine pasture, carpeted with all manner of colourful flowers and ferns. It is an almost level walk at first, followed by a gentle ascent for about two kilometres till one arrives at a saddle on the ridge. At an altitude of about 3,950 metres, this is the highest point of the trek and also forms the watershed between the Sainj and Tirthan valleys. From this point the trail drops sharply and veers to the south-east. One is required to negotiate a succession of deep watercourses coming from the left; fortunately, they are all completely covered with snow and ice during the winters, and one can just walk across the snow bridges. The terrain is undulating for most part of the trek barring one spot, which is quite risky: one has to traverse the face of a cliff on a ledge that is barely 18 inches wide, and the fall to one's right is of about a thousand feet. This would be troublesome to cross even in the summers, but in the winters, with the ledge coated with ice, one should be doubly careful. Once across, it is again a gentle descent to the campsite at Guntarao, which is basically a spot on the left flank of a ridge extending in an East–West direction, about 100 metres below the ridgeline. (The ridge back itself is too windy and exposed to set up camp, hence the preference for this location). There used to be a forest hut here, but it was blasted by lightning some years ago and all that remains of it now are a few burnt logs. We therefore pitched our tents next to it and spent the evening gazing at the myriad glaciers and snowfields to the east.

The second day's trek takes one to Rolla on the banks of the Tirthan. Initially one climbs about 200 metres to a point called Rakhundi Top, situated at an altitude of 3,660 metres. This is a windswept, rocky crest where the weather changes suddenly and the rain hits one horizontally. It is best to cross it as quickly as one can: we were caught in a thunder squall and had to take ineffective shelter in the lee of some rocks, there being no trees as the saddle is high above the treeline. The sun broke through after about half an hour and we left happily; we discovered much later that one of the party had left his camera and wristwatch behind one of the rocks (he never did explain why he had felt it necessary to take off his watch!). That evening one

of our porters was sent back to look for them. He was able to retrieve the watch but the camera was never found, or so we were told. It was probably sold to some unsuspecting tourist in Manali a few days later! From Rakhundi Top it is a continuous descent through thick forests for about two hours till another pasture called Shilt (3,100 metres). Shilt is a relatively good campsite with a wooden hut but does not have any source of fresh water. From here it is about two hours' descent to the forest department's trekking camp at Rolla on the right bank of the Tirthan. Trekkers coming from the Guntarao side do not stop here for the night as Rolla is within reach, but those doing this trek from the Tirthan end need to stop here to take a break from the 1,000-metre climb from Rolla. We pressed on to Rolla and some minimal comforts of civilisation—log cabins, running water, wooden floors, and cooked food. The next day one proceeds on the left bank of the Tirthan for about two hours to the roadhead at Gushaini, and continues on to Sai Ropa and Kullu, or Mandi, on national highway 21. This trek completes the journey from Sainj valley to Tirthan valley. However, both Rakhundi Top and Shilt receive a lot of snow in the winters, as a result of which the trail can become quite risky. Hence, it is advisable to check the snowfall and weather before venturing on this route. Likely wildlife sightings include the ghoral, musk deer, monal, and tragopan. To trek in the GHNP one has to obtain permits from the director of the park, whose offices are located in Shamshi on the main Mandi–Manali national highway, about 10 km before Kullu. The park administration makes all arrangements for porters, guides, equipment, etc. at very reasonable rates through a community-based organisation (CBO) called SAHARA. Reservations for the various camps and forest huts can also be made with them. The number of trekkers allowed is restricted so as not exceed the carrying capacity of the park, and hence it is advisable to make reservations in advance.

The Great Himalayan National Park was declared a World Heritage Site by the UNESCO in July 2014.

2002

FACING PAGE:
Author's son Saurabh at Rakhundi Top

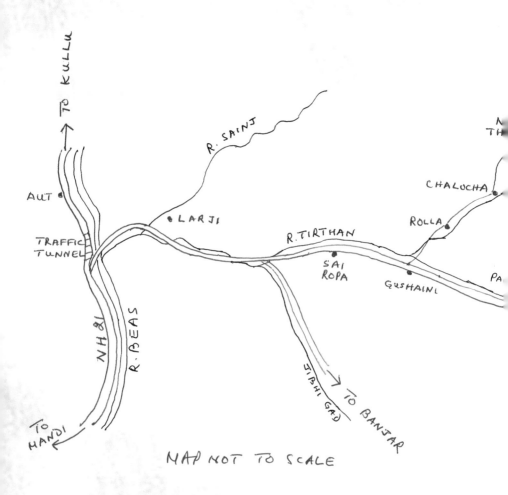

N

TO KULLU

R. SAINJ

CHALUCHA

AUT

LARJI

ROLLA

TRAFFIC
TUNNEL

R. TIRTHAN

PA

SAI
ROPA

GUSHAINI

NH 81

R. BEAS

JIBHI GAD

TO BANJAR

TO
MANDI

MAP NOT TO SCALE

= MOTORABLE ROAD
— TREKKING ROUTE
• VILLAGE/CAMPING SITE
— RIVER/STREAM
• GLACIER

Tirath
THE GLACIER AND
THE BLUE SHEEP

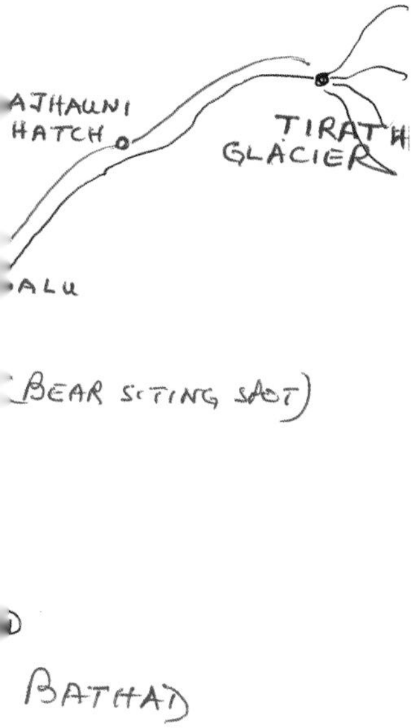

AJHAUNI
HATCH

TIRATH
GLACIER

ALU

BEAR SITING SPOT

BATHAD

The Tirthan is one of four streams which drain the 754 sq. km of pristine temperate Himalayan forests and high altitude pastures that comprise the Great Himalayan National Park (GHNP) in Kullu district; the others being the Parbati, Sainj, and Jivanal. Flowing in a north-east to south-west direction and meeting the Beas at Aut, about eight kilometres below on the Mandi–Kullu national highway, the Tirthan is a quintessential mountain stream. Born at 4,500 metres from the womb of the Tirath glacier on the eastern fringes of the GHNP, it cascades down through snowfields, pastures, and dense forests— unbelievably varied terrain that is home to the blue sheep, brown bear, and the western tragopan. The river itself, at least in its upper reaches, is one of the very few in the state that can still boast of running trout. More importantly, it has been spared the ravages of hydel projects that have claimed and destroyed the ecosystems of all other major rivers in the state—Sutlej, Ravi, Beas, Giri, Pabbar, Parbati, and Sainj. For this reason alone Tirthan valley is a trekker's and nature lover's delight. The real complete trek is to the source of the river, the Tirath glacier. Our little group had been to the respective sources of the other three streams in the GHNP, and in 2008, we decided to complete our own version of the *char dham* by going to Tirath.

Since the entire trek is within the boundaries of the GHNP, it was organised by the GHNP administration through a CBO called SAHARA; in fact, no other body or agency is permitted to organise journeys within the park. SAHARA is a CBO whose members consist of families affected by the creation of the GHNP, which did lead to partial loss of livelihood options—grazing cattle in the park forests, extraction of medicinal plants and firewood, hunting etc., all of which are now banned. The CBO was therefore created with the help of the park administration to provide alternative livelihood options. Organising treks within the park is only one of these activities and provides employment to about 50–80 youth for roughly 100 days in a year. It is a good system: the rates are fixed by the GHNP administration, the members of SAHARA—who also serve as porters, guides, and cooks on the expeditions—are all screened by and known to the administration, and the visitor is guaranteed a safe, well-organised trek at reasonable rates. For large groups or groups that demand more than the basic arrangements, SAHARA ties up with a couple of private tour organisers in Kullu or Manali, but even these must have the approval of GHNP.

The recommended base for the Tirthan trek—and the one which we opted for—is the large GHNP trekking-cum-training complex at a place called Sai Ropa, situated on the left bank of the Tirthan at a height of 1,440 metres, about an hour's drive from Aut. It has a very well-appointed two-room rest house, a two-room researchers' hut, and dormitories for more than 50 persons. Scattered along this idyllic single-lane road by the river are a number of private lodges, camping sites, and even homestay units, which are being vigorously promoted by the tourism department as an alternative to the mess that urban tourism has become in the state. These are not high-budget or high-end places but are reasonably priced with decent accommodations and good food, including local Himachali cuisine. Not all who stay in these places venture into the GHNP; most are content with short walks, river crossing, angling, or just lazing in these pure, undisturbed environs. Since we were going into the core of the park on a five-day trek, we preferred to stay in Sai Ropa where we could be in touch with the rest of our large team and the GHNP administration.

Day one begins with a short, four-kilometre drive up the river to Gushaini, a collection of shops and the last provisioning centre for those going into the park. It's a four-kilometre level walk from here to the tiny village of Ropa, via the two even tinier villages of Shilinga and Kharancho. At Ropa, a wooden gate announces the entry proper to the GHNP. There is a small office and a two-room hut here, and was being developed by the forest department as an ecotourism site with tenting platforms, toilets, etc. at the time of our visit; a good idea since Ropa is at an ideal distance from the roadhead for those who would like to camp out for a night or two without having to undergo the rigours of a trek. One interesting and telling thing we noticed was that while the river was brown and silt-laden till Ropa, upstream of it the waters turned a lovely bluish-green within a couple of hundred yards! This was due to the fact that there were no controls on land cutting, agriculture, or road construction below Ropa, whereas upstream the territory of the park began and no non-forestry activity of any type was permitted there. Maintenance of green cover was the only explanation for this phenomenon and therein lies a big lesson for the administrators of this state. The walk beyond Ropa is much more enjoyable thanks to the tree growth, which is much thicker, and the absence of villages in this valley: when the park was created, all private rights and lands within its area were acquired by the government and the people fully compensated. Only the villages of Shakti and Marour in the Sainj valley remain to be relocated. But even in Tirthan valley one wizened old man is holding out. Chande Ram looks at least 75 years old (but is probably 65) and owns about 10 bighas (10,000 sq. metres) of land in the park. The government had deposited the compensation for his estate with the district collector 20 years ago, but Chande Ram refuses to accept this amount and continues to occupy his land. While the park administration figures out a solution to this impasse, the gutsy old man continues to till his land within the boundaries of a national park, growing potatoes and peas, and no doubt indulging in a little poaching and equally illegal extraction of medicinal plants on the side! He lives alone but for two fierce mongrels that ensure that no forester gets too close to his house. He graciously made tea for us (and the forest officials accompanying us!) and maintained that his presence there was actually in the interest of the department because he ensured that no illegal activity took place in the area!

About one kilometre from Ropa the track crosses over to the right bank of the Tirthan over a wooden bridge, and after another three kilometres one arrives at Rolla, a well-appointed camping site on the banks of, and perched just above, the river at a height of 2,100 metres. It consists of two large huts (one with an attached toilet and running water!) that can accommodate 20 persons. If needed, there is ample space outside to pitch tents. Both banks of the river are heavily wooded; animals come down at sunset to drink from the river and we were lucky enough to spot two ghorals that evening. We spent a pleasant night around a campfire, listening to the steady murmur of the river and the night calls of the forest denizens.

Day two involves a gruelling ascent and its best to start latest by 8:00 am. There are two trekking options from here. The first, of course, is the one we were taking: straight up the river to its source at the Tirath glacier. The second is to leave the valley immediately after Rolla and climb in a north-west direction to the gorgeous pastures of Shilt, on to Guntarao, Rakhundi Top, Dhela Thatch, and then down into the Sainj River valley and the village of Shakti—a three-day trek from the valley of one river to another. We picked the first course as we had already done the trek to Sainj valley some years ago. Our destination was Nada Thatch, 12 km away and 1,200 metres higher up. Still on the right bank of the Tirthan, the track gets narrower and progressively worse, most of it washed away in a massive flood in this river in 2005. The track follows a north-east alignment and the area across the river is known as Khorli Poi. (*Khorli* means "hollow" and *poi* means "trunk". The place is named after a huge hollow deodar tree next to the track in which 20 persons can fit comfortably!) We could see vast thatches (openings in the forest in which sheep herders—Gaddis—camp with their herds), and amazingly dense and multi-hued forests of deodar, blue pine, and broad-leafed species such as prunus (wild jamun), alder, moru oak, aesculus, alnus, and rhododendron. The mix of colours and hues would be difficult to capture in any camera because each species has its own distinct hue—from the dark and fresh green to the brown, russet, and downright red. Beyond these splendid colours lies the famous Jalori Pass (3,135 metres), on the ridgeline that divides the watersheds of the Sutlej and Beas basins. Khorli Poi is prime habitat for the western tragopan pheasant (the symbol of the GHNP and also the state bird), which roosts in the low-slung rhododendrons and forages in the hill bamboo and undergrowth. Precisely for this reason the park administration does not allow trekkers in the Khorli Poi area as a general rule.

After four kilometres one comes to a place called Chalocha, distinguished by a huge deodar tree that is worshipped as the abode of two local *devtas*—Kala devta and Chunjwala devta. The latter has now shifted to Bali Chowki in the neighbouring district of Mandi where an annual fair is held in his honour. It is a local custom for worshippers to embed pieces of iron, ranging from nails to axe-heads to even clothes hangers, into this holy tree, which is consequently festooned with these shining objects. It is also customary to pray to the *devta* who resides here before beginning the long climb to the glacier. The climb to Nada Thatch (3,333 metres) actually starts from here—1,200 metres of unremitting ascent over about eight kilometres and through dense forests. As we steadily gained altitude the massive peaks of Asurbagh on the other side of the river rose into view, covered with snow even in the month of May. After climbing for three hours, we emerged without warning onto a huge glade. The Nada Thatch is large as thatches go: about five hectares in size, it slopes gently eastwards towards the river, which flows about 100 metres below. It is surrounded by a luxuriant growth of kharsu (brown oak), giving way to fir and spruce on the higher slopes. The edges of the thatch sported clumps of dwarf rhododendrons that had just finished flowering. The thatch itself was completely carpeted with knee-high growth of *Rumex nepalensis*. This

A moonlit night over Nada Thatch is a weed which grows in nitrogenous soil and was indicative of the fact that this area had been heavily grazed by goats of the Gaddis in the past, whose urine introduced nitrogen into the soil. The weed had completely displaced whatever flowers or herbs might have flourished here earlier and exemplified the effects of human disturbance in these pristine areas. *Rumex* usually grows in conjunction with a nettle called *bichu booti*—literally scorpion grass—which has sharp spikes that cause excruciating pain and itching (though it's not poisonous). This nettle had also established itself in the glade. Interestingly, nature has made an effort to atone for this vicious creation: alongside the *bichu booti* one can invariably find another plant called *palak*. This is a long-leaved plant or grass about six inches high. Its leaves, when crushed and applied on the spot where the skin has come in contact with the nettle, provide immediate relief and are an effective, locally available antidote.

We pitched our tents in the thatch and were woken up just before dawn by the most amazing symphony of bird calls. But the first call I heard, surprisingly, was that of a barking deer at about 4:30 am. It circled the campsite from a distance, barking enquiringly the entire time, and then there was silence. I was surprised because this high altitude is not the habitat of the barking deer, and this particular deer was certainly at the extreme edge of its range. Barely had the barking deer left when the birds took over in an opera of music conveying, like nothing else could, the sheer joy of living and welcoming the arrival of another brand new day. First were two western tragopans with their slightly grating calls, very similar to the hoarse wailing of a baby; next were the monals with their much more mellifluous calls, both alarmed and inquiring; then came the minivets with their busy, no nonsense chatter. I just lay in my tent, listening to these exuberant musicians of the natural world who rejoiced in a similar manner with the arrival of each new day, happy to have survived the night and not knowing what the coming day had in store for them. There is so much we humans can learn from this simple philosophy of life, I thought, caught in our complex web of desires, aspirations, possessions, fears, and ambitions. Be grateful for each new day that God gives you and expect nothing more. If you can sing again the next dawn, do so; if you can't, so be it. At least you sang his praises yesterday and rejoiced in whatever time he gave you in this beautiful world.

By about 6:30 am it was full light and the avian orchestra had long fallen silent. On this third day we had to proceed to the next campsite at Majhauni Thatch, 14 km away and at a height of 3,600 metres. The track initially descends about 500 metres through dense forests of maple, rhododendron, and *Taxus baccata* (yew) to the river. At one point we unwittingly rousted at least a dozen monals from the undergrowth. Some we saw, the presence of others we could surmise by the loud and distinctive fluttering and whistling sounds as they took off—not the most elegant of flights. The forest was brimming with all kinds of birdlife. We could not see them but could hear their continuous calls— monal, leaf warbler, nutcracker. We even came across a troop of about 20 langur monkeys who kept a wary eye on us from their high perches on the trees. After about two kilometres on a winding, gently graded track, one comes to a sloping grassy clearing surrounded by massive

Taxus and maple trees. We measured one of these *Taxus* trees and found that it had a girth of 14 feet! This was Hada Thatch. From here the path suddenly dips into a nullah, a rocky watercourse fed by a waterfall further up. The going here is extremely difficult because one has to make one's way through cascading waters and over slippery rocks, all at an angle of about 70 degrees. The vertical distance is 250 metres and it has to be negotiated using nothing but all four limbs and a stout stick. However, we had a most unexpected surprise at the bottom!

The narrow, precipitous watercourse gradually flattened out into a fairly broad (about 50-metre wide) glade. The stream flowed through the middle of this glade with huge rocks and boulders scattered on either side. Sitting on one of these boulders was a female Himalayan black bear! She was supremely oblivious to the presence of the 15 or so open-mouthed members of our party and lay unperturbed on the rock, bathing herself in the warmth of the morning sun. She

A surprised Himalayan black bear below Hada Thatch

appeared to be pregnant, which might have been the reason for her passive behaviour for black bears are notoriously aggressive, especially when surprised by human intruders. Also, bears have spectacularly poor vision and it is quite possible that she could not initially sight us. The sound of a dozen people clambering down the watercourse must also have been drowned out by the muted roar of the fast flowing waters, preventing her from hearing us either. Consequently, for a full 10 minutes she presented us with an amazing photo op. Direction of the wind must have changed then, wafting our scent to her, for she suddenly stood up, bounded across the stream to its left bank, scaled a sheer 10-metre-high rock face with no effort at all, and disappeared into the thick vegetation. I personally could not believe my luck because in my 15 years of trekking in the remotest parts of Himachal, this was my first sighting of a Himalayan black bear. It augurs well for the park too since her behaviour indicated that perhaps she was not too used to human presence in these forests, as otherwise her reaction might have been different. I wish her and her cub all the luck—may she and her progeny rule this part of paradise forever.

After a gentle descent of about a kilometre the track meets up with the Tirthan again, coming from the east, at a spot called Balu. Across the river are pristine forests and high pastures sans any habitation, which is a birdwatcher's delight; a recent census conducted in that area established the presence of 35 to 40 western tragopans there, an extremely good density. Wisely enough, no trekkers are allowed in that part of the park. This area is referred to as Asurbagh or Devil's Garden, which even the Pandavas are supposed to have avoided! The whole Tirthan valley, in fact, is replete with myths of the legendary Pandavas, who are supposed to have stayed for some time in this valley during their exile—these myths only add to the richness of this region.

The track now veers east, going upstream along the right bank of the Tirthan. It is ill-defined and broken, plunging and climbing crazily; all that remains of the track that was washed away in a massive flood in 2005. In fact, the original track from Rolla hugged the river all the way to Balu, completely bypassing Nada Thatch and obviating the strenuous climb to the latter. But the 2005 flood completely washed away this stretch, which is now too dangerous to use, and the park administration is not too inclined to restore the original track; the idea is to make the trek as difficult as possible so as to discourage all but the most committed nature lover! I'm afraid I cannot disagree with this line of reasoning: the biodiversity of these forests is very fragile and cannot sustain many footprints. It is a gruelling eight kilometres from Balu to the next camping site at Majhauni Thatch (3,600 metres). The track initially negotiates up and around huge boulders along the riverbank, which is tiring and occasionally risky. One's footing has to be sure and one also has to judge correctly on which rock to put one's weight—some of them look huge and solid but are often precariously balanced and can tip over due to a trekker's weight. A fall here can only result in broken bones; one should be extremely careful and not try and break any speed records! Landslides have obliterated the track at many places, forcing one to leave the riverbank and climb above and around them. The worst of them occurs roughly a kilometre from Balu: it is about 300 metres long and 200 metres high—too big to bypass; we had to clamber along its face, 100 metres above the frothing river. We virtually had to carve our footholds along the 60-degree face, foot by foot, anchored only by one foot and a stout walking stick to prevent us from sliding down as the surface consisted of precariously perched rocks on loose shale. There can be no permanent track here and every trekking party has to repeat this exercise as it takes only slight rainfall to wash away the efforts of the previous party.

Finally, after four kilometres or so the track veers away from the river and climbs about 300 metres into dense woods. But the tiring up-and-down routine continues unabated because of the many streams flowing down to the river from the north. There were numerous bear and some leopard scats along the trail; we were happy to see them since they were a clear indication that bears were thriving in the area. They were most probably black bear because the larger and more aggressive brown bear is not a denizen of the forests and prefers the high pastures at altitudes of 9,000–10,000 feet. We reached Majhauni Thatch six hours after leaving Nada Thatch. Much smaller than the latter, Majhauni Thatch is located at a very narrow point in the river valley; it was very windy and cold here because wind from the now nearby Tirath glacier scythes down this funnel-like feature, usually accompanied by rain in the afternoons. Fortunately, there are three cave overhangs here, one of them big enough to accommodate at least 10 sleeping men. These make for very good shelters in bad weather and are ideal as all-weather kitchens because the cooking fires can keep going even in the heaviest of rains! The vegetation around this thatch is extremely interesting: the steep slopes to the left or north (which is the southern or south-facing aspect) consist almost entirely of kharsu or brown oak. Across the Tirthan on the northern aspect was a dense growth of *bhojpatra* or birch, the broad white leaves of which still command religious significance as the writings of sages in ancient times were inscribed on them. The russet hues of the oak provided magnificent contrast to the freshly washed green of the birch. The birch forests, and the rich undergrowth it supports, provide an ideal habitat for the shy and reclusive musk deer. Incidentally, some members of our party were lucky enough to sight one at 5:00 am the next day—it crossed the river over a snow bridge, meandered through our campsite, and disappeared into the kharsu forests to the north. We spent an hour looking for it but, not surprisingly, never saw even a sign of it. The musk deer, which is about the size of a small goat, is one of the most endangered animals in the state. Though very shy and elusive it is easy to poach for those who know its habits and the terrain. One extraordinary trait makes it very vulnerable: the musk deer always defecates at one chosen spot within its territory; if there are other musk deer in that area they also use the same spot—a kind of community latrine! All that an experienced poacher has to do is to locate this spot and lie in wait for the poor unsuspecting creatures to come there, as they inevitably will. The state forest department, with the help of the central zoo authority, is planning to establish a breeding centre for the musk deer at Kufri, near Shimla. But the department has little technical expertise in this area and its experience

with a similar centre for the western tragopan at Sarahan does not hold out much hope for the success of this project.

The night at Majhauni Thatch was not very comfortable as it rained intermittently throughout the night and the tents were cold. We tried lighting a fire under the larger overhang but the gusts of freezing wind soon made us give up that idea. However, dawn on this fourth day arrived bright and sunny. There was an air of palpable excitement in the camp since this was the day we were to go to Tirath glacier itself—source of the lovely Tirthan River we had been following for the last three days. It was not only because of the religious significance of the journey—the source is considered a major pilgrimage spot for the locals—but primarily because the glacier and its surrounding snow fields and mountain slopes are prime habitat for the rarely sighted bharal or blue sheep. There were scattered but confirmed reports of a few rare sightings in the last few years and we were keen to check them out. The snow leopard also prowls this region—the blue sheep his stock prey—but none of us even remotely expected to spot this mythical predator of ice and snow; just being in his fiefdom was stirring enough for us. But the blue sheep we certainly expected to see!

The distance from Majhauni Thatch to Tirath is about eight kilometres, but it takes at least three hours to cover as there is practically no trail except for the last two kilometres or so. Initially we went on the Tirthan itself—on huge ice or snow bridges, some a hundred metres long, which had formed on and across the river. These are very interesting natural formations: the river here flows along a gorge with high banks on either side, which were covered with thick deposits of snow and ice. These deposits, under their own weight, slide into and over the river, completely covering it with a frozen cover of ice that can be a few feet thick. The river continues to flow under this ice and it is a sight to behold—the gushing waters disappearing suddenly into a gaping black hole and emerging again a hundred metres downstream in a white welter of foam and spray. The ice bridges provide a convenient trail to walk along, but one's footing must be sure and one should stay in the middle where the ice is thickest. Towards the edges the ice-cover

PAGES 78-79:
Trekking
party standing
on the frozen
Tirthan River
(author in blue
jacket)

is thinner and may not support a man's weight. Crashing through and into the waters is not an option; one would either freeze to death within minutes in the sub-zero waters or/and be dragged under the ice bridge and wedged against a submerged rock by the swift current, and inevitably drowned. These ice bridges on the Tirthan last till about the end of May in a typical year and then melt away. While they last, however, they provide a good highway and a means for animals to cross the river conveniently!

A typical ice bridge on the Tirthan River

We covered the first two kilometres on these ice bridges; these formations then disappeared and we climbed into the forests on the right bank where the trail meanders through rockfalls, landslips, and watercourses—not an easy stretch to negotiate. However, after about six kilometres of this labour, the valley broadens out to about half a kilometre and the trees give way to lush green pastures carpeted with the most astonishing variety of pure alpine flowers and ferns. The mosaic of colours that they create—purple, blue, red, yellow, white, mauve—has to be seen to be believed, and for us this was indeed the pot of gold at the end of the rainbow! Interspersed among the flowers were a host of rare medicinal plants and herbs. We almost felt guilty treading on these lovely flowers, but such was the sheer profusion of this floral wealth that there was no other way across this unending pasture! The backdrop to this pasture is equally magnificent—straight ahead to the east and south-east rise high, snow-capped peaks and ranges, behind which lie the forbidding Srikhand massif and the ranges of Sarahan. On their flanks are huge glaciers and snowfields; the melt-off from these form a myriad of tiny black ribbons which appear to braid the upper valley like falling ringlets on the alabaster bosom of some fair Nordic beauty. This melt-off converges into two primary streams, which, on reaching the valley floor, join to form the infant Tirthan, which then flows down the pastures in the direction we had come from. Some distance to the right

A panoramic view of the Tirath snowfields. A cluster of blue sheep can be seen in the middle distance

of this is a small circular pool of water about 20 feet in diameter, again fed by two slim channels of snowmelt. On the floor of this pool, which is about five feet deep, are two small circular depressions from which one can see spirals of gas or air rising. The locals believe that it is this pool, and not the stream mentioned earlier, which is the true source of the Tirthan. It does not really matter because the outflow from this pool joins the stream a few score yards further down and this magnificent river is born. As per tradition we all performed a small puja or prayer near the pool and took a hasty dip in the stream—the cloud cover and the bone-chilling winds streaming off the glaciers just a few hundred metres away ensured that there was no frolicking in the waters.

Just as we finished putting back on our clothes the cloud cover on the massif ahead of us lifted, the sun lit up the mountains, and straight ahead on the snowfields, high above on the mountain flanks, we spotted a herd of at least 40 bharal or blue sheep! To its right was a second group of another 30 or so bharal. This was an unbelievable sighting since this extremely elusive alpine goat is rarely seen in such large numbers. They were climbing straight up the mountain, across the snowfields and glaciers; it appeared to us that the herds had been feeding on the pastures when we arrived and, disturbed by our unexpected presence, had retreated up the mountain slopes, a terrain where they had no match (except perhaps for the snow leopard). The bharal continued climbing the sheer slopes without any effort, and when they were about a thousand feet above us they stopped and surveyed us. They were in no hurry—this was their domain, the ice and snow they had made their home and where only they knew how to survive. We were the puny interlopers who could only gawk at this magnificent landscape for a few hours before having to return to the comforts of "civilisation". Sooner rather than later the bharal would reclaim these pastures. And sure enough, conscious of the fact that the day was drawing to a close and it was a three-hour hike back to camp, we had to retrace our steps back to Majhauni Thatch. The bharal watched us go in silence.

2011

N

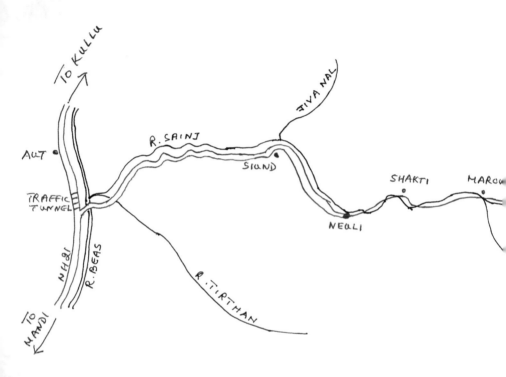

TO KULLU

JIVA NAL

R. SAINJ

AUT

SIUND

SHAKTI

MARCU

TRAFFIC
TUNNEL

NEULI

NH21

R. BEAS

R. TIRTHAN

TO
MANDI

MAP NOT TO SCALE

══ MOTORABLE ROAD

── TREKKING ROUTE

● VILLAGE / CAMPING SITE

── RIVER / STREAM

● GLACIER

Rakti-Sar
THE GLACIAL WOMB

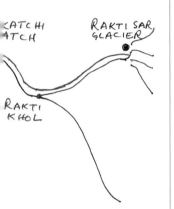

The Sainj is one of the tributaries of river Beas and meets the latter on its left bank at a small village called Larji, about 25 km below Kullu. Flowing through the Great Himalayan National Park (GHNP) for most of its course, the Sainj originates deep inside the park from the Rakti-Sar glacier at 4,000 metres. Tracing its route to this source translates into one of the most fascinating trekking experiences a nature lover can wish for. In fact, to borrow a spiritual phrase from Hinduism, for us this was the third of the four *dhams* that comprise the naturalist's *char dham* of the GHNP: going to the respective sources of the four wonderful streams flowing through the GHNP—the Parbati, Jivanal, Sainj, and Tirthan—all meeting the Beas within a stretch of 20 km between Bhuntar and Larji.

As is usual for the GHNP's high-altitude treks, the best time is from mid-June to end-September; we did it in June. Crossing over to the left bank of the Beas at Aut, we drove to Larji where the Sainj and the even more beautiful Tirthan meet. Leaving the Tirthan here we advanced up the Sainj valley in a roughly easterly direction to Sainj village, about 14 km away. The hub of all activities of the Parbati Hydel Project in this valley, the village is now a semi-urban sprawl and has completely lost its rural charm. It is not a place where one should tarry. About 10 km beyond it is Siund where construction of a powerhouse was in full swing for the first phase of the Parbati Project; it is here that the waters of the Parbati and Jivanal were to be dropped into the Sainj to produce 800 MW of power. We could see the openings of three huge penstock tunnels on the right bank of the river, on which all greenery had been desecrated in a huge swathe. In fact, the entire hillside had become an artificial structure, grouted as it had been with thousands of tons of concrete. Many more tons of debris was being dumped into the river itself, turning its waters into a muddy welter. (About a month after we passed through this place the inevitable happened: the entire hillside collapsed on the tunnels, pushing the entire project schedule back by many months and crores of rupees; of course, nobody has even thought of assessing the damage to the environment or revising the designs/plans to make them more environment friendly). Siund is no longer a place to linger at and we quickly left, driving another six kilometres upstream to Neuli where the road ends. Comprising almost entirely of a few shops, dhabas, and tiny guest houses, Neuli is the gateway to the GHNP in this valley; by now we could not wait to get off the MUVs and take off on foot.

It is 22 km from Neuli to Shakti, the first day's camping spot, and one could not ask for more pleasant hiking conditions. The well-marked and wide trail faithfully sticks to the Sainj, first on its left bank, criss-crossing a couple of times over wooden bridges that sometimes tilt alarmingly, and ending up on its right bank. Thick forests cover both banks, coming right down to the water's edge. Within a couple of kilometres of leaving Neuli the waters return to their original clear texture, the angry roar at Siund transforming into the happy, gurgling, rock-splashing music of a typical mountain stream. For the first six kilometres or so one is in the ecozone area of the GHNP, and thereafter one enters the Sainj Wildlife Sanctuary, which continues up to Shakti. There are only three or four tiny settlements between Neuli and Shakti: Niharani, Denga, Chenga, and Baha, out of which the first couple are doomed. Even though this entire area falls within the ecozone of the GHNP, the state government has approved a 100-MW hydel project (the Sainj HEP) slated to come up at Niharani, about eight kilometres inside the zone. The diversion dam shall inundate large parts of the forests and agricultural fields here; it is horrifying to think that within a few years this splendid spot shall become like Siund. The sanctioning of this project, despite the directives of the Supreme Court and the laws on protecting national parks and wildlife sanctuaries, is symbolic of the complete failure of all governmental systems—political, administrative, and even judicial—in this country. The devastating consequences of setting up such a project on the fringe of this protected area shall be felt for many years to come. However, the resilience and ingenuity of the villagers is demonstrated here in a novel manner. We saw an entire row of bare skeletal frames of buildings which had recently come up on the right bank at Niharani, like a hollow film set. On enquiring we were informed that since the government would soon be acquiring all the land and buildings here for the project, these frame structures would be shown as full-fledged buildings for the purposes of claiming compensation! Lakhs of rupees would be claimed for structures costing just a few thousand, and since the assessment would be done by notoriously obliging government engineers, there was a lot of money to be made. We frankly did not grudge the villagers this—they would be losing for ever a way of life; if they made some money out of this, it was in no way more than what they deserved!

Shakti is a small village comprising about 25 houses on the right bank of the Sainj; about half a kilometre before the village is the trekkers' camp—a basic but functional complex of two rooms, a dormitory, a kitchen, and toilets with running water diverted from a little stream behind it. The camp has no electricity but has a thoughtful fire pit in front where very welcome bonfires can be lit in the evenings, which can get quite chilly. The camp is situated in the middle of a thick grove of sea buckthorn trees, their pervading green broken only by the shocking red of poppies in the flower beds. There is absolute tranquillity here, which is only reinforced, surprisingly, by the continuous roar of the river, barely 50 metres away. We spent a very restful night here.

Day two involves a 20-km trek to Parkatchi Thatch and so it is best to leave not later than 8:00 am. We carried packed lunch with us, cooked the night before in order to save time. Leaving camp we crossed the river to the left bank over a new wooden bridge—the last one was washed away in a flash flood the previous year. We were following the Sainj eastwards; to the south and south-east lay the vast expanse of the GHNP, mile upon mile of pristine forests all the way to the massive peaks of the Srikhand range. Our first staging point was Marour, the last hamlet in the valley, eight kilometres away: the trek to Marour was similar to that of the previous day, ascending gently through dark forests spattered with sunlight. The opposite bank, being south-facing, had sparser vegetation and we were lucky enough to spot two ghorals coming down to the river for a drink. We watched them for about five minutes; they must have heard us for they disappeared behind some bushes and we did not see them again. We reached Marour in about two hours. This small hamlet of about 10 houses is located on the right bank of the river and is accessed by another wooden bridge. It is situated at the confluence of the Sainj and another substantial stream coming down from the south. Marour has nothing of particular interest to recommend it except an ancient temple—there is no sign of any government here and the residents aren't too friendly either. The park administration is wary of the villagers, suspecting them of poaching, illegal extraction of medicinal herbs and plants, and grazing of sheep and goats in the park area, which is prohibited. There used to be a forest hut here but one winter's night a couple of years ago it mysteriously went up in flames; the authorities are confident that it was deliberately torched by the villagers in order to discourage visits by the forest guards and rangers. All that remains now is one dilapidated shed and the stone chimney, pointing an accusing finger at the sky. This has been a loss not only for the forest staff but also for trekkers. Fortunately, recognising the trekking potential of this area, the tourism department has now sanctioned 10 lakh rupees for constructing a trekkers' camp here on the same lines as Shakti. (This camp is now ready and functional).

We lunched near the remains of the forest hut and pressed on. Initially one has to walk along the sandy, rock-strewn river bed, which is quite wide here (a good place to pick up driftwood!). The track then starts climbing, winding its way north-eastwards through thick, waist-high undergrowth. The going is not easy and one has the choice of two trails. The first one meanders through the forest, about 500 feet above the river, going up and down, in and out of nullahs, occasionally making wide detours around huge landslides. Quite often there is no visible trail and one has to just flounder along in a general north-east direction. The second track is entirely along the river bed. However, it is not as easy as it sounds for one has to jump from one rock to another, a tiring process that also involves a certain amount of risk. At some points the river bank is so precipitous that one has to leave the river, climb to higher ground, and come down again when the terrain

Campsite at Parkatchi Thatch

permits. Not much of a choice. Half of our party took the upper route while the other half took the river route—at the end both were cursing just as loudly! It is about 10 km from Marour to Parkatchi. On the last stretch one has to cross another huge stream coming from the north; this is the Chiush Nullah and it appears to carry almost the same volume of water as the Sainj. It is crossed over a wooden bridge and immediately after is a very steep ascent. Just when you think the climb will never end, the dense forest of fir and spruce suddenly parts and before one's unbelieving eyes appears a huge, luxuriant, flat meadow, framed by forests on three sides and an untouched mountain range on the fourth. This is Parkatchi Thatch.

A "thatch" is a high-altitude meadow that is generally used by shepherds—Gujjars or Gaddis—as camping grounds. Parkatchi Thatch also used to serve this purpose till about two years ago when grazing was banned by the park authorities. (Incidentally, the Chiush Nullah, which we crossed earlier, is the boundary between Sainj Wildlife Sanctuary and the GHNP. Parkatchi Thatch resides within the park). The decision to ban grazing in the national park was not an easy one to take, according to the director of the park, Sanjeeva Pandey, who was part of our team. Hundreds of families derived livelihood from the 20,000-odd sheep and goats they reared and grazed in the forests and pastures comprising the park. But the whole idea of creating the GHNP was to retain its natural biodiversity with zero human intervention, and this could not happen as long as tens of thousands of these animals were allowed to freely roam the area. They caused immense damage to the plant life, both by their grazing and by their mere presence. At places where the sheep clustered (such as in the thatches) their urine made the soil extra nitrogenous, encouraging the growth of weeds and grasses that stifled and smothered the natural plant life. Indigenous species were being replaced by exotic ones. This was especially disastrous for the scores of rare and valuable medicinal plants that the park is rich in. The domesticated animals could also be carriers of diseases that the wild animals have no immunity against. The very presence of humans in large numbers caused severe stress to the notoriously shy wildlife

of these temperate forests and even disturbed their breeding cycles. *A cobra*
And finally, under the garb of shepherding, the villagers would indulge *plant—notice*
the hood from
in rampant poaching and extraction of medicinal plants; hence the *which it gets*
decision to ban grazing or ingress of sheep and goats into the park *its name*
area. The result became evident to all of us over the next few days,
even though only two years had passed since the decision was taken.
Parkatchi Thatch itself was replete with luxuriant, waist-high vegetation
whereas earlier (we were told by the accompanying forest staff) it used
to be grazed to the ground during this pre-monsoon period. We also
counted hundreds of the rarest Himalayan medicinal herbs growing
right there—the Salam Panja (*Dactylorhiza hatagirea*), whose roots look

just like the palm and five fingers of a child; Ratanjot (*Arnebia*), which is used to cure dandruff and as a hair dye, and many others that only an expert would recognise. Sanjeeva Pandey conducted a sample count on the thatch and found to be the density of Ratanjot was about 800 plants per hectare (it would be even more in the surrounding hills, pristine and undisturbed compared to the thatch). Even he was pleasantly surprised by this high figure which, according to him, indicated that these once-threatened species were making a slow but distinct comeback now that grazing had been stopped. We would see further confirmation of this on our trek to the glacier the next day.

Parkatchi Thatch is situated on a huge, protruding bluff about 300 feet above the river and at a height of 2,950 metres. About the size of four football fields, it is completely surrounded by thick stands of fir and spruce. To the south is the river itself and to the north the hills rise steeply beyond the treeline. Towards the north-west one can see, barely a couple of kilometres away, the high, snow-covered peaks from which the Chiush stream originates. All this, incidentally, is prime brown bear and western tragopan habitat, and we could see signs of the former everywhere. Bears are notoriously lazy creatures and, in order to save energy, like following trails and tracks left by humans or goats rather than making their own. We saw at least seven brown bear scats on the trail from Marour, indicating that they were present here in good numbers. To the east (up the Sainj valley) loomed the massive, rounded, ice-covered peak of Munda Tapra, at least 6,000 metres in height; beyond it lies the Rampur area of Shimla district. However, given the height of the range and the fact that it is covered with perennial ice, no one has ever been able to cross over from this side. The entire thatch was carpeted with a luxuriant growth of yellow euphorbia flowers, interspersed by bright patches of red primula and blue geraniums with the purple of Ratanjot ferrules standing out here and there. No landscape artist could ever have visualised the mix of colours that we had the privilege to see. There is a two-roomed wooden hut on the western edge of the thatch, built a couple of years ago by the forest department, but we preferred to pitch our tents in the middle of the meadow. On the eastern end are a couple of huge rocks, so positioned that they make the perfect kitchen. The only problem is the absence of a water source in the thatch and the same has to be fetched from a trickle about 200 metres away to the east. The park administration is now considering laying an HDPE pipe embedded under the ground (so that it doesn't freeze during winters) from the Chiush Nullah, about a kilometre away, and bringing the water to the campsite using gravity—a feasible idea and not an expensive one. It rained lightly that night but not enough to worry us.

Day three dawned with a fair cloud cover. It is about seven kilometres to the Rakti-Sar glacier (14 km round trip) over difficult terrain and hence we left camp at 6:00 am after just a cup of tea, carrying packed lunch with us. For the first couple of kilometres the track heads due east through thick vegetation above the river, the dome of Munda Tapra dominating the distance. It then comes to a junction where a large stream from the south-east joins the Sainj: this is Rakti-Kol, a simple, small collection of rocks with prayer flags atop, identifying it as a Devi temple where travellers pay obeisance before moving on. The Sainj turns sharply to the left (north-east) here and almost immediately the character of the track changes. It practically disappears in the dense undergrowth; the bank of the river for large stretches is too eroded to offer any footholds and one has to constantly slither up and down. It used to be much better, but a couple of years ago there were floods in the river and the track was washed away. Moreover, when goats were allowed in the park the movement of hundreds of these animals kept the track well-defined and free of vegetation; now that they no longer come here, nature is gradually reclaiming its own. The park authorities are not particularly keen to do anything about repairing the track as that would only encourage the shepherds to come back quietly! One needs to have a good guide or one can get lost in the bushes and boulders bordering the river. We carefully negotiated a couple of huge landslides and three ice bridges, each about 50 metres wide. We found tracks of blue sheep (locally referred to as *maitu*) on the sandy edges of the stream—they come down to drink in the late evenings and early mornings, and then disappear into the high crags on either side.

After about two hours of difficult and not-very-enjoyable hiking we came to a large thatch, or rather a succession of thatches, and the walk became easier. The valley broadens out and the peaks above Rakti-Sar now come into view—mighty, snow-capped domes completely shutting out the head of the valley to the north-east. The lush meadow we were now walking through was about 500 metres wide and with a myriad ribbons of water threading it. The valley walls were about 300 metres high on either side: to our left they were rocky and bare; in sharp contrast the walls on our right, facing north, were covered with thick clusters of fir and spruce. If one is lucky one can spot the occasional monal pheasant taking flight and gliding gracefully down the valley with the typical whistling sound of its wings. Soon, the relentless climb takes one above the treeline; however, the meadow is carpeted almost knee high with the most incredible variety of grasses, alpine flowers of all shapes and hues, and a bewildering array of rare herbs and plants. It is difficult not to agree with Sanjeeva's theory that

The alpine pastures above Rakti-Kol

Rakti-Sar glacier—source of the Sainj River. Its snout can be seen in the middle distance

the absence of sheep flocks has made a massive difference to the flora of these alpine regions.

After wading through this vegetative abundance for two kilometres, we followed the valley as it curved slightly to the left; straight in front we could see the snout of a massive, horseshoe-shaped glacier—the source of the river Sainj. It must have been 40 feet high at the leading edge and was completely covered with dark grey moraine. From its toe emerged the sparkling waters of the Sainj. The glacier itself and its accumulation zone stretched back into the massive ice slopes, merging with the mighty mountains that were its source, their crests completely shrouded by clouds. At least 17,000 feet high, these unnamed peaks have never been scaled as far as anybody knows. Just looking at this one montage of nature made me feel utterly humbled by its purity, its timelessness, its splendid isolation, its complete unconcern with anything to do with humankind—after all, these mountains and these snows had been here millions of years before the precursors of man slithered out of the oceans! The stream we saw, however, is not regarded as the Sainj by local people. There is a high ridge of moraine running straight down from the snout of the glacier, and at right angles to it, for about 250 metres. The stream we could see flows down the left side of this ridge (as you look up). But on the right side is a fairly large, rectangular depression or bowl through which flows another, much smaller ribbon of water, also emerging from the glacier snout. This ribbon branches out into a number of channels which flow through the depression, round the edge of the ridge, and go on to join the first stream to finally form one waterway. It is this ribbon of water that is revered by the locals as the real Sainj—they call it Rakti-Sar. In all probability and according to the tale the villagers here believe, two events that occurred in the distant past perhaps explain why the main channel is not considered the real Sainj. The locals recount that the face, or snout, of the glacier was originally much wider and fed its stream into the bowl on the right side of the moraine ridge, forming a holy lake. (The bowl, in fact, does look very much like the dried up bed of a lake). The ridge of moraine was also much longer, almost completely damming up the stream and enabling the formation of the holy lake

A rudimentary shrine near the snout of the glacier

behind it. Then, perhaps hundreds or even thousands of years ago, two events occurred that changed this frozen landscape entirely. First, the right side of the glacier's snout (as you look up) broke off and fell into the lake. The snowmelt thereafter stemmed only from the left side of the snout, resulting in the flow to the lake practically drying up and creating the stream on the left we see today. At about the same time, maybe because of the sudden tidal force of thousands of tonnes of glacial ice falling into the lake, the lower part of the moraine ridge gave way and the waters of the lake drained away, leaving only the narrow channel seen today, fed by the remaining trickle from the snout, *the Rakti-Sar*. The villagers revere this small channel and not the wider stream, and have erected a small cairn of stones on the ridge—the *jogni*—complete with prayer flags and incense sticks; every visitor to this sacred spot prays to it. In fact, to reach the ridge and the Rakti-Sar one has to cross the combined stream below the ridge. No footwear is allowed beyond this point and the remaining journey to the bowl and the *jogni* must be completed barefoot! The really devout perform a complete *parikrama* of the lake bed.

Rakti-Sar means, literally, "head covered with blood". The mythology of this remote vale has it that a powerful *rakshasa* or demon known as Raktibeej lived in the surrounding mountains during ancient times. He had received a *vardan* or blessing that made him practically immortal—each time a drop of his blood fell on the ground a new Raktibeej would spawn from that drop. Secure and confident in his invincibility he began to rival the gods themselves. There was little the gods could do because the *vardan*, once bestowed, could not be revoked. Finally, in desperation, the gods dispatched the mighty Goddess Mahakali or Shakti to vanquish Raktibeej. Mahakali caught hold of the demon with two of her hands, chopped off his head with her third hand, and in the fourth, held a vessel into which the blood from his severed head was collected. Since no blood was spilled on the ground, the demon could not resurrect himself and perished. As proof of this legend the locals indicate a small stretch of the stream which emerges from under a rocky outcrop, red in colour! This epic battle is supposed to have taken place in the bowl beyond the ridge and this is how the little stream gets its name—just one of the incredible myths that this land abounds in, connecting man, nature, and God.

It was two in the afternoon by the time we reached Rakti-Sar and it had started to snow rather heavily. We tarried for some time at this sacred spot, performed our pujas at the *jogni*, had a quick lunch, took some photos, and departed as it was a long, five-hour trek back to Parkatchi Thatch. But not before Sanjeeva's son had the incredible good fortune of spotting a brown bear on top of the glacier snout! The bear emerged from behind a rock, stood up tall on its hind legs to get a good look at us, didn't like what it saw, and made off up the glacier at a clip! We reached back at our campsite after dark, spent the next day basking in the thatch, and returned to Shakti the day after, exhausted but elated at having been to the source of one of the most beautiful rivers in the state.

2008

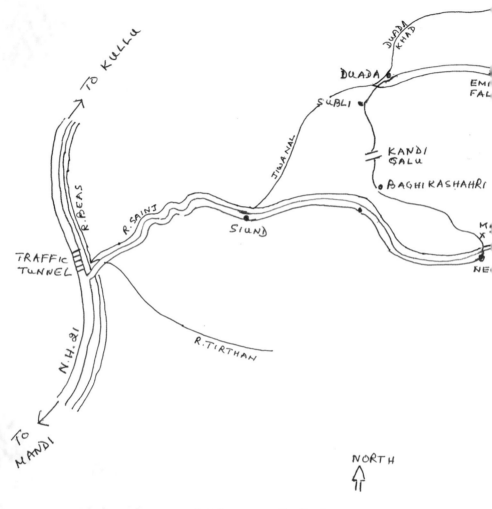

TO KULLU

DUADA KHAD

DUADA

SUBLI

EMI
FAL

JIWA NAIL

KANDI
GALU

BAGHI KASHAHRI

R.BEAS

R.SAINJ

SIUND

M.
X

TRAFFIC
TUNNEL

NE

N.H.21

R.TIRTHAN

TO
MANDI

NORTH
⇑

MAP NOT TO SCALE
═══ MOTORABLE ROAD
── TREKKING ROUTE
● VILLAGE/CAMPING SITE
── RIVER/STREAM
≋ GLACIER/SNOW FIELD
═ PASS

Jivanal

RTU GLACIAL POND

SARTU
CAMPSITE

SATOGANI GALLU

SATOGANI
THATCH

SHAKTI

The Jivanal (or Jiva Nullah) is the third major stream in the Great Himalayan National Park in Kullu district. It drains the north-western and western sides of the park: flowing first in a westerly and then south-westerly direction, it is only about 65 km long and debouches into the Sainj at Siund, about 10 km below Neuli. The Jivanal valley and catchment area comprise probably the most remote and interior areas of the park, completely devoid of any habitation, and offer fascinating possibilities for trekkers. One of the best routes, which takes one right through the core of the western part of the park, is up the Sainj valley, across the ridgeline to the north-west and into Jivanal valley, down the river for a couple of days and then back into Sainj valley. It takes seven days of strenuous hiking where the descent is just as demanding as the ascent, but every minute of it is worth it for the sheer range of terrain and landscape is unbelievable.

On the first day one drives up the Sainj valley from Aut to Neuli (26 km). En route one passes Siund, about 10 km before Neuli, where the Jivanal meets the Sainj. This is also the place where the powerhouse for the Parbati Stage-II (800 MW) is being constructed. It is an ambitious engineering

A precarious track along the Sainj River venture by which the waters of the Parbati (west of the Jivanal) will be routed south-eastwards through an underground headrace tunnel (HRT) and dropped into the Sainj at Siund to generate 800 MW of power. Along the way the waters of the Jivanal shall also be tapped and diverted into the HRT; consequently, once the project is complete, the present confluence at Siund would practically cease to exist. The road from Aut to Neuli, once a picturesque single-lane, has now completely been devastated as it is being ruthlessly widened to enable heavy machinery for the project to ply. Lakhs of cubic metres of earth and debris are being thoughtlessly shovelled into the Sainj River in complete disregard of all environmental considerations. The state government conveniently looks the other way, its myopic gaze focused on the 12 per cent free power that it would get from the project.

Thankfully, upstream of Siund normalcy is restored since there are no project activities here. (This was true in 2007 when we had undertaken this trek. Unfortunately, since then the Sainj HEP has received all clearances and excavation work has started on it in full earnest about a kilometre above Neuli. I was shocked to see the devastation being caused when I visited the area again in 2010). The road ends at Neuli and we were actually grateful for the chance to get out of the vehicle, shoulder our rucksacks, and start walking. It's a 25-km walk to Shakti, largely through the ecozone area of the GHNP and entirely along the Sainj. Neuli is at an altitude of 1,500 metres and Shakti is at 2,100 metres: the ascent of 600 metres over 25 km is quite gentle; the track is generally level with a couple of fairly steep ascents. On the way one crosses the tiny hamlets of Niharani (four houses), where the Himachal Pradesh State Electricity Board (HPSEB) has received approvals for the Sainj HEP, a 100-MW project on which preliminary work has started; Baha (5 km); and Chenga (7 km), which boasts of three houses and a broken-down forest hut.

Site for the powerhouse of the Parbati project at Siund. Notice how the green hillside has been converted into a concrete face!

Chenga's claim to fame, however, is its *up-pradhan* (deputy of the village headman) who goes by the name Jai Sriram and has eight wives. We all wanted to meet this remarkable man to learn how he managed eight of them when we could barely cope with one, but unfortunately for us he was not home! We saw a number of birds typical of the area: the tiny plumbeous water redstart with its startling red bottom skimming the river in search of fish and insects, the amazing brown dipper which dived under the waters for as long as 15 to 20 seconds, and the barbet with its provocative calls. The track, initially on the left bank of the river, keeps criss-crossing the stream. After about 12 km one enters the Sainj Wildlife Sanctuary on the right bank and remains within it all the way to Shakti—a fairly large village by the standards of the area with about 20 houses and a primary school. It is the second last village in the Sainj valley; about three hours further upstream is the last village known as Marour (which, however, does not lie on the route of this trek). Shakti has a well-organised trekkers' camp run by the park authorities: it has dormitories, three double rooms, kitchens, running water, and toilets. It has no electricity but there is a proposal to harness a small waterfall just behind the camp by installing a portable generator to produce 5 kW of power. We spent a comfortable night here, not deterred by the knowledge that this was the last opportunity for a shave and a bath for the next seven days!

The second day is one of the toughest of the trek, involving a climb of 1,600 metres to Satogani Thatch (3,700 metres) over a distance of 15 km. One leaves the Sainj immediately after Shakti and turns left (north), past a temple and a cave that used to house the local primary school before a building was constructed for it a couple of years ago. The unremitting climb begins immediately and lasts for seven hours. There is no discernible track as there are no settlements on this route anymore; only the occasional hardy shepherd wanders this way with his flocks. At this time of the year (July) the undergrowth is thick and wet, coming up to one's armpits, and one has to proceed cautiously as the slope is quite steep. The vegetation too is dense, broad leaves first giving way to conifers and then to kharsu oak and hill bamboo, known

as *nirgal*. Once high above the Sainj, across the river one can see the magnificently coloured forests of the Dhela escarpment. Dhela Thatch is clearly visible on top of the opposite ridgeline—a long, light-green clearing amongst the surrounding forests. The continuous ascent is very steep and exhausting, and it is a relief when, after about seven hours, the ridgeline is attained. Breaking free of the trees, one is confronted with a magnificent meadow that stretches east to west for three or four kilometres. The path now turns left (west) along the meadow, following a small stream that is a tributary of the Sainj. The entire meadow was blanketed ankle-deep in flowers and we were to have the privilege of walking through them for the next two days: blue geraniums, Himalayan blue poppies, Brahma Kamals, red primulas, and yellow-tinted geums.

The "hippo" rock in the Sainj River. Remarkable resemblance!

Happily coexisting with these flowers was a whole range of rare medicinal plants and herbs: *dhoop*, *karu*, *patish*, *hathpanja* (*Dactylorhiza*), and the white anaphloes—all contributing to the amazing medley of colours. In all my days of trekking I had never seen such richness and profusion of colours; a testimony to the fact that when human access is limited, Nature bounces back with all the fecundity at its command. This beautiful place is known as Satogani Thatch.

We set camp on this pasture next to a *dogri*, a small igloo-like structure built only of stones, about four feet high. *Dogris* are the standard shelters of shepherds—made of stones since no wood is available at these heights, they are very practical. The overlapping stone slabs do not allow any wind or rain to enter inside and the structure can withstand the heaviest snowfalls; even if they get covered with snow they will not collapse under the weight. This particular *dogri* was deserted, but some fuel wood was lying around and it appeared to have been vacated by its owner just a couple of days ago. This area is part of the Sainj sanctuary and grazing here is prohibited. Our party included the director of the GHNP (under whose jurisdiction the Sainj Wildlife Sanctuary falls) and his staff, and it was quite apparent that word of his visit had somehow reached the shepherd(s) who must have gathered their flocks and climbed high above the pasture. No doubt they kept a keen eye on us and returned to their *dogri* the moment we left the place! It drizzled that night but not enough to disturb us.

Day three dawned bright and clear: clouds were nestled in the valley below us like fluffs of wool; the towering peaks to the north were bathed in orange and gold by the rising sun. Our trek for the day would span about seven hours and take us to Sartu. Although Sartu is only about 15 km away and at a height of 3,700 metres, getting there involves crossing the Satogani Pass. From the camping site the track, or what there was of it, headed due north-west through the pasture. The first four kilometres or so are fairly level, followed by a steep climb of 200 metres to a ridge called Bali Gallu, the base of the pass. From here, a fairly gentle ascent of about 250 metres brings one to the pass called Satogani Gallu (4,300 metres). Before the actual pass is a deceptive ridgeline about 50 metres below, which may look like the pass itself but is not. It is important to note this because the lower ridge is still in the Sainj catchment in a North–South axis; if one were to start descending from there in the mistaken belief that it was the main pass, one would descend westwards and circle back towards Satogani Thatch! The main pass lies due north-west of the lower ridgeline, about 15 minutes away over boulder-strewn terrain and about 50 metres higher up. It is not usually visible from the ridge since it is around a corner, as it were. It is on a south-west–north-east axis. There is a small glacier on the other side followed by a rockfall, neither of which is difficult to negotiate. The track then heads due north through lush pastures and along a little stream (originating from the same glacier we had just crossed) for four kilometres—one is now in the Jivanal catchment and back in the GHNP. At this point one is not actually in the valley of the Jivanal (which lies on an East–West axis) but on a kind of shelf. After about four more kilometres this shelf drops steeply into the actual Jivanal valley from its south. Far below, about 250 metres, one can see the slender ribbon of this mysterious river flowing from east to west (from one's right to left as one approaches it from the Satogani Gallu) at an almost perfect right angle. Beyond the river and to the north, the valley is walled in by massive ramparts of the Khandadar massif, rising to more than 18,000 feet, beyond which lies the Parbati valley. The eastern end is closed in by even higher mountains, rising to more than 20,000 feet, and even at the end of July one can clearly see huge glaciers on its western slopes, from which originates the Jivanal; beyond these peaks is Spiti. One can cross the Khandadar from Jivanal valley to reach Parbati valley by an extremely difficult trek, emerging at Pulga, about 20 km upstream of Manikaran. But as far as I know there is no established passage from this valley to Spiti over its eastern ramparts.

Dropping down from the shelf, we reached the Jivanal at about four in the afternoon—too late to ford the river as both its volume and current had risen with the melting of snow during the day. We therefore pitched our camp on the nearer side of the river (left bank).

We were disheartened to see a huge flock of a couple hundred sheep grazing on the other side. Although grazing in the park is completely prohibited, the administration has to wage a constant battle against the shepherds; a battle which, with their scanty, ill-equipped, and generally lethargic staff, they appear to be losing. This is a major sociological problem and dilemma: the shepherds have known no other way of life for centuries and cannot easily switch to some other profession in an area where employment opportunities are hard to come by. So they persevere with their age-old practice, encouraged by the typical vote-centric Indian politician who, instead of lobbying with the government for a rehabilitation or resettlement plan for these nomads, is only interested in cheap populism and vote-picking. Keeping the Indian politician company here are a few NGOs and self-proclaimed CBOs who are ever-ready to fish in troubled waters, and see in this whole imbroglio an opportunity to make a name and perhaps impress some foreign donors.

The camping site is a huge field, half a kilometre long and a hundred metres wide, completely carpeted with flowers of every conceivable colour. Little streamlets flowing down from the Satogani ridge add to the sylvan beauty. There is, however, no wood available as the site is still above the treeline; the nearest clump of trees is five kilometres down the Jivanal valley. It's also extremely windy here with the cold wind blowing straight up the valley. The wind however drops by about 8:00 pm. One can see a couple of makeshift wood-and-stone *dogris* or huts of the shepherds, the latter known locally as *fuals*—a generic term for all high-altitude shepherds in Himachal. That evening we ran out of most of our rations as the party which was supposed to come up the valley from Bhagikashahri with provisions did not arrive till very late at night. Moreover, they were on the other (right) bank of the river and obviously could not cross it. We had only some pulses left *(arhar dal)* and were lucky enough to be able to purchase some wheat flour from the offending shepherd whose sheep were illegally grazing there! That night we ate what is locally called *siddu*—cakes of kneaded flour paste boiled in water and eaten with the dal. It's quite tasty and very nutritious.

If one is not pressed for time one should spend a rest day at Sartu; we did, basking in the warm sunshine, drying our clothes, just soaking in the magnificent landscape with its medley of sounds, colours, and fragrances. One can take a leisurely walk up the valley towards the glaciers and snowfields that are the source of the Jivanal. If one is lucky one can even spot wildlife, for this is the territory of the ghoral, the tahr, and the massive Himalayan brown bear. We ourselves were unable to sight any wildlife but this is purely a matter of chance and luck for, unlike their subtropical brethren, the temperate or Himalayan fauna is extremely shy and elusive, and can be practically invisible at such high altitudes.

Campsite at Sartu. The infant Jivanal can be seen emerging from the mountains

On the fifth day, we had to go from the Sartu camping site to Subli (3,400 metres) about 15 km away, most of it down the Jivanal valley. The first step, of course, is to cross the river itself, which means camp must be struck latest by 7:00 am as the first rays of the sun hit the glaciers much earlier. Since the camp is barely a few kilometres from these glaciers, it does not take the melting snows very long to reach Sartu and for the river to swell. At this time of the day the waters are about thigh deep, but very fast and biting cold. It is not dangerous unless one were to lose one's footing on the slippery rocks; it's best to form a chain of three or four persons and cross as quickly as possible. It doesn't take more than two minutes for your legs to become completely numb, and you better be on the other side before that happens! After the crossing the track veers left (west) and follows the river downstream for 10 km. Before that, however, just half a kilometre from the crossing point is the Sartu glacial pond, a sparkling, blindingly blue emerald embedded in this rocky grassland—a perfect pendant for the garland of glaciers all round. About 200 metres in circumference, it is silently fed by two small trickles of water from the high mountains at the back. So still and clear are the waters that the reflections on it are near perfect. The pond is in a small, bowl-like depression and thus, is also an ideal camping site.

Reluctantly leaving this gem of nature, we continued down the right bank of the Jivanal for another 10 km along a fairly easy track. We encountered some spectacular snow bridges and waterfalls on the way. While photographing one of these waterfalls one member of our party, a young French girl called Emily, stumbled and fell. We promptly named this particular waterfall as "Emily Falls"! After 10 km we reached Duada, the literal meaning of which is "where two paths meet". And that is exactly what happens here—a major khad (gorge) called the Duada Khad meets the Jivanal from the north. This Duada Khad is the route to the Parbati valley: going up this khad one comes to a pasture known as Lahul Bati, beyond which is the Phanchi Gallu (4,646 metres). This is the boundary of the national park and Parbati valley lies on the other side. This is an extremely arduous two-day trek and must not be attempted unless one is in peak physical condition; full logistical support including guides must be obtained from the park administration.

Duada itself is just a clearing next to the river, surrounded by thick forests of fir, spruce, and the kharsu oak. There is no habitation here except for a broken-down trekkers' hut. One can, however, discern the faint ruins of an old village on a nearby knoll, and there is an amazing story behind these ruins. Local legend has it that about 150 years ago, Duada was a thriving village of sixty or so houses. The local *devta* or god allowed the villagers to live here on the condition that they are not to kill the animals or birds in the forests. After some time, however, the villagers of Duada ignored this covenant with the *devta* and started slaughtering the wildlife. The furious deity emerged from the forests one night, pulled down all the houses, killed each and every villager, and buried them in the ruins of their own huts. Not surprisingly, no one has dared to establish a settlement here again—the ruins are a stark reminder of what had happened to those who attempted to do so on the last occasion. The local *devtas* are all-powerful in these remote regions where no other formalised or institutionalised religions exist, and the villagers obey their diktats implicitly. Practically every valley has its own "resident *devta*", probably because in these difficult areas (where even today there are no roads and basic amenities are hard to come by) inter-valley communication in earlier days was virtually non-existent. The Jivanal *devta* rules with an iron hand, as we too experienced first-hand. He has forbidden the consumption of meat or eggs in the valley—as a result our provisions party coming up from Bhagikashahri, which had been carrying a few dozen eggs at our special request, had to leave them at Sainj. The *devta* has also forbidden the entry of any lower-caste people into the valley from outside; a couple of our porters, therefore, also had to stay back.

Duada is a good place to break for lunch for after this is a steep climb to Subli (3,400 metres), about five kilometres away. One kilometre downstream from Duada, we crossed over to the left bank of the Jivanal on a *dhippi*—a thick log thrown over the stream and weighted down with heavy stone slabs. Once on the left bank the track gradually snakes upwards in a south-west direction, leaving the river and climbing up the walls of the valley. This climb of about 300 metres

Jivanal valley is accomplished in three stages, all of which are along watercourses that are usually dry. We, of course, were caught in heavy rains and had to ascend against the flowing waters. Dense forests envelope the track the entire way; half way up is a huge meadow that looks like a Darjeeling tea garden, so perfect are its contours! It takes two hours to reach Subli, which is basically a large clearing in the forest facing westwards. It has a big but broken-down patrolling hut and enough space to pitch four or five tents. The campsite has adequate water and dense clumps of rhododendron encircle the area: this is ideal monal and tragopan territory and we heard them clearly in the evening, though we could not sight them. It was particularly heartening to hear the tragopan because it is a creature of the primeval, virgin forests; it cannot survive in any other kind of environment. If there is any disturbance in its habitat it stops breeding and, in a few years, vanishes forever. Its presence is an indication that the forest environment is healthy and untouched—on hearing its cries we silently thanked the *devta* of Jivanal!

On the sixth day we awoke at 5:00 am to the most amazing orchestra of bird calls; minivets, barbets, nutcrackers, thrushes, choughs— all serenading the sunrise in an amazing, uninhibited, unforgettable performance of sheer joy and innocence. One could ask for no better music with one's bed-tea! This would be the longest day of trekking so one should leave early. Heading due south and climbing about 300 metres, it took us an hour to reach Kandi Gallu (3,700 metres), the pass on the ridgeline between Sainj and Jivanal valleys. Beyond Kandi Gallu lies the catchment of the river Sainj; the ridge also forms the boundary of the GHNP—beyond it lies the ecozone area of the park. From Kandi Gallu, which is a narrow, craggy saddle, we could see on the far ridges the villages of Shensor and Bhagikashahri, the latter being our camping point for the day. The whole area is magnificently forested and kindles the hope that maybe, just maybe, we will succeed in preserving these jungles and all they contain for our grandchildren, and for posterity; it is unthinkable that they shall never lay eyes on these marvels of natural evolution.

From Kandi Gallu there is a fearsome descent of 1,100 metres over just six kilometres to the Shensor Khad or Guddam Gad. The descent is unremitting; the track is very steep and hardly ever defined for the first couple of kilometres. It weaves through rockfalls, ravines, gulleys, and along precipices, almost completely hidden at this time of the year by long grasses and undergrowth. One has to be extremely cautious every step of the way. After some time rhododendron clumps begin to appear followed by oak. After about four hours, just when one's knees are about to give way, one reaches the Guddam Gad at 2,600 metres: a small, elegant stream with a pool of crystal clear water, just begging one to fling off the clothes and take a dip! This area would make a wonderful camping site if one has the time; in any case it is a good spot to take a lunch break, for it is still a gruelling 10-km hike to Bhagikashahri.

The track from Guddam Gad to Bhagikashahri continues to move in a southerly direction through dense forests, but it is a tortuous one— going in and out, up and down ravines, across precipitous slopes, and there are at least three points that can be considered perilous. It is best to travel in a group. All in all it's a very tiring walk and raises the age-old dilemma for conservationists: should these tracks be improved by the park administration to make them safer? That would make it possible for more trekkers to come to these remote places. But the director of GHNP, Sanjeeva Pandey, who was also part of our group, was vehemently opposed to this. His reasoning is that these virgin areas are extremely fragile and already subjected to great biotic pressures by the shepherds and local villagers. Their ecology cannot sustain the pressures of a large number of visitors, especially as the typical Indian trekker or tourist is not known for his sensitivity to the environment. Therefore, the park management should not intervene in the natural processes in virgin areas such as the Jivanal valley, and should certainly not do anything to attract larger numbers here. Given the state of things, according to him, only the true nature lover would take on the difficulties and risks of a trek to these regions, and Mr Pandey would not like any other type of visitor to come here. There are other areas of the park where the treks are easier and they are welcome to those parts. I must confess that I find a lot of logic in what he says.

The trek from Guddam Gad to the little village of Bhagikashahri takes about three hours. Just before the village is a huge clearing with the ruins of an ancient settlement: this is a *devasthan* or holy place. The village was earlier located here, but for some reason was shifted to its present location a kilometre ahead many years ago. This is now considered a sacred place with a small temple where all travellers on this route pause to pay obeisance to the deity by blowing on a conch shell that is kept in the temple for the purpose. In fact, one interesting point we noted was that all the settlements or villages en route this trek had their own *devasthan* or sacred groves. Since these spots belonged to the local *devta* or deity, the trees there were fully protected and no one dared fell or even lop these trees, or even graze their cattle in these areas. As a result, these groves were lush with thick vegetative growth and home to a myriad species of birds—a firm indicator of the fact that our forefathers were not averse to mixing religion with conservation. In fact, just about every local *devta* I've heard of in all my years of trekking in these remote mountains have decreed strict rules for the protection of the forests and wildlife within their jurisdictions; a conservation code that has stood the test of time. It is only in recent years, with the intrusion of politics, crass commerce, and outsiders that the code has been violated. The flavour in fashion today, unfortunately, is a mix of religion and politics. I much prefer the earlier mix of religion and environment!

Bhagikashahri has about 20 houses scattered over a fairly large area. Since it is not connected by road, its only economic activity is

The Manu temple at Bhagikashahri

agriculture. But it has electricity and a well-constructed primary school with about two dozen students. We camped for the night in the grounds of the school itself.

The next day was the eighth and last day of the trek. We would come full circle today and arrive back at the Sainj, which we had left six days ago. It is about 12 km to Sainj, a level walk for the first nine kilometres through fields of corn, rajmash, and other vegetables. It is hot here for one is now down to an altitude of 6,000 feet. The track moves in a south-south-easterly direction and after about nine kilometres suddenly ends on the lip of a deep valley, at the bottom of which flows the Sainj River. We were now almost directly above the township of Sainj whose glistening corrugated tin roofs were spread out a thousand feet below. At the starting point of the descent is located one of the most unusual temples one has seen: this is the Manu temple dedicated to Manu Rishi, author of the sometimes controversial ancient text *Manusmriti*. I am not aware of any other temple dedicated to this sage, but the peculiarity of this temple is not limited to this aspect alone. The Manu temple is a magnificent edifice, built in the shape of a pagoda! Its central support is provided by the trunk of a massive dead tree and around it are wrapped layers upon layers of the pagoda-roofed structure. The architecture of this temple is ample proof of the fact that the influence of Buddhism in Himachal was not limited only to the tribal districts of Lahaul-Spiti and Kinnaur. However, it remains a mystery as to why it did not take more permanent roots in these valleys. Perhaps the hold of the local *devtas* was too strong. Perhaps the appeal of the *devta* was more relevant to the residents of these difficult, remote regions, for whom religion had to postulate a more practical, worldly approach to life and provide a bulwark against the forces and furies of nature rather than a philosophical approach to life. Whatever be the explanation, the Manu temple is a priceless aspect of our heritage and is held in great veneration in these parts. A serai in its spacious compound provides for a good camping site.

From the temple, it is a sharp thousand-foot descent to Sainj, basically along a steep, rocky watercourse. This aspect of the slope is south-facing and therefore, baking hot during the day. It is best to cover this last leg either early in the morning or late in the evening. It takes about 40 minutes to reach the right bank of the Sainj River, which is crossed over an old log bridge; a new, steel bridge is under construction. On the left bank is the motorable road taking one back to Aut and the Mandi–Manali highway. As we climbed back onto our waiting vehicles, we looked up to our right—high up on the distant ridgeline was the silhouette of the Manu temple, an upraised finger exhorting us to remember that fascinating worlds and civilisations exist even beyond the highways.

2007

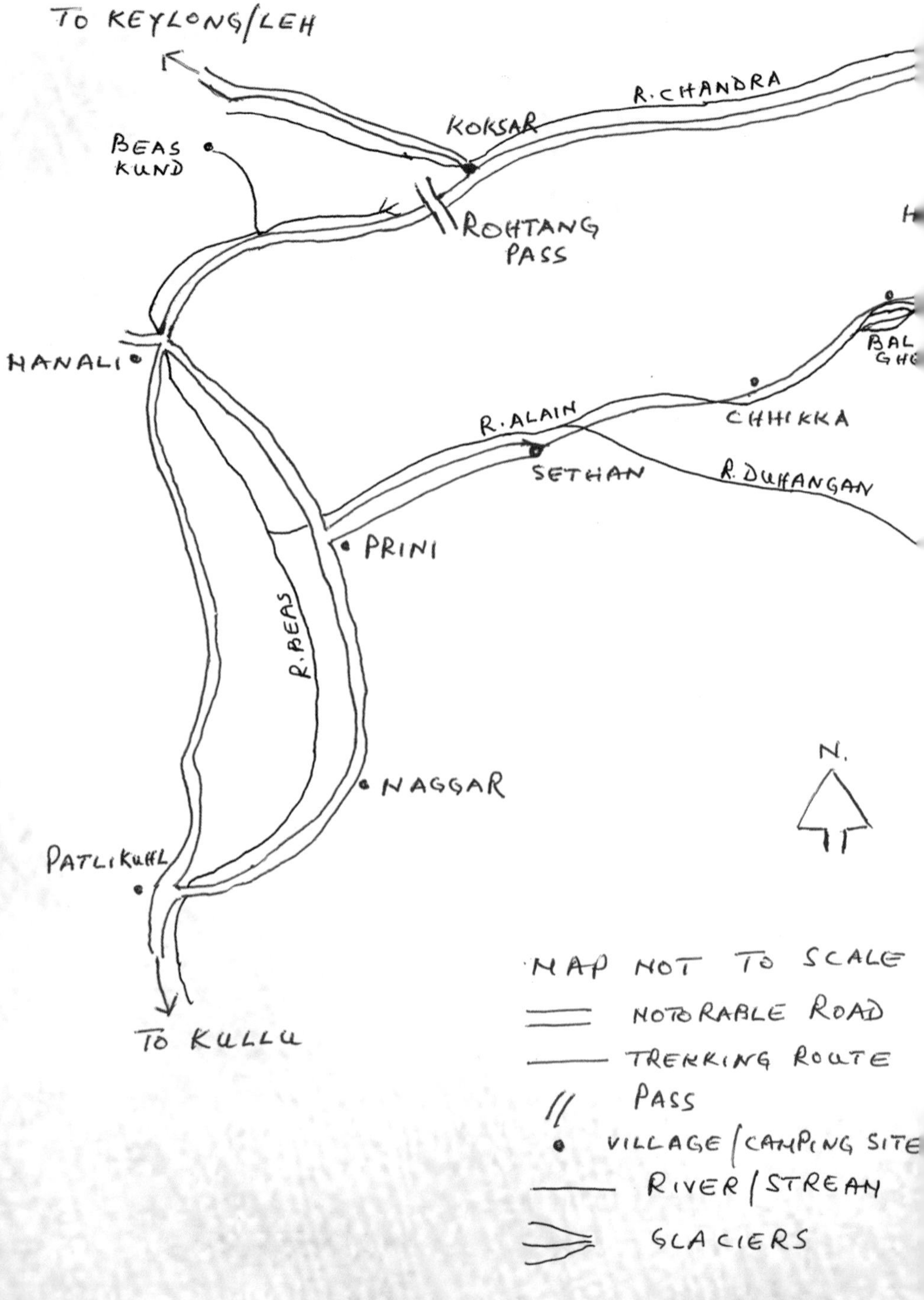

TO KEYLONG/LEH

R. CHANDRA

KOKSAR

BEAS KUND

ROHTANG PASS

HANALI

BAL GHE

R. ALAIN

CHHIKKA

SETHAN

R. DUHANGAN

PRINI

R. PEAS

N.

NAGGAR

PATLIKUHL

TO KULLU

MAP NOT TO SCALE
═══ MOTORABLE ROAD
─── TREKKING ROUTE
// PASS
• VILLAGE/CAMPING SITE
─── RIVER/STREAM
⟩ GLACIERS

ATRU TO KUNZUH
PASS | KAZA

GLACIERS
HAMTA
STREAM

N THALI

GLACIERS

Hamta-Pass

The massive Pir Panjal range of the Greater Himalayas in Himachal stretches in a line from the west-north-west to the east-south-east, dividing the districts of Lahaul-Spiti and Kullu. Impregnable as it looks, the range is dotted with high passes all along its length that have been used by the local people, especially the shepherds, for centuries. With the ever-increasing network of motorable roads, these routes and their passes have fallen into disuse and are now traversed almost exclusively by the nomadic Gaddis and shepherds. However, they offer fascinating and challenging treks, and the chance to witness at close quarters the unrivalled landscape of the Greater Himalayas. Starting from the north-west, the passes are: Kugti, Chobia, Kalicho, Rohtang, Hamta, and Pin Parbat. The first four primarily served the Lahaul area while the latter two were used by residents of the Spiti area for crossing over to Kullu district.

Hamta Pass (4,227 metres), about 300 metres higher than Rohtang, is one of the lowest and most accessible of the whole lot. Before a road was built over the Rohtang, the route over the Hamta was the standard passage from Manali to Spiti—this is the shortest line between the Beas and Chandra rivers. A fairly popular trek now, it used to start from the small but prosperous village of Prini, about five kilometres below Manali on the left bank of the Beas. Dotted with apple orchards and guest houses in equal number, this once pretty village has now been immortalised as the domicile of Atal Bihari Vajpayee, former prime minister of India. Mr Vajpayee has built a cottage here and comes to visit at least once every year. He loves to mingle with the local folks who have unreservedly adopted him in typical Himachali fashion, notwithstanding the inconveniences they are put to by the SPG and local police whenever Vajpayee visits. The Alain stream joins the Beas at Prini from the left (north); the original trek route went straight up the Alain valley, climbing steeply through a thick deodar forest, past the villages of Sethan, Kharmdiari, Sarotu, Jabri, and on to Chhikka. But all that has changed now as a consequence of a large hydel project coming up at this place. The 192-MW Alain Duhangan Project shall trap the waters of the Alain and Duhangan (a similar sized stream to the east of the Alain) high above Sethan, and bring their combined waters down to Prini, where a power station will generate about 800 million units of electricity every year. To carry the required men and materials for the project, a 12-km road has been constructed up to a place called Jabri where the forebay tank shall be located, completely despoiling the first part of the trek.

Instead of trekking up to Sethan, therefore, we drove up the project road, which winds its way up in a succession of steep hairpin bends through what was once a dense deodar forest. The road has devastated the forest and dozens of trees have been felled; more shall inevitably fall in the years to come as a result of the digging and excavation. The view of the Beas valley from here, however, is awe-inspiring—the whole of Manali and Prini are laid out far below as if on a toposheet, dotted with a myriad orchards, the gleaming ribbon of the river meandering lazily among them. After climbing for about eight kilometres we reached a huge, level ground—a clearing in the forest—of about 12 hectares. This is known as the "potato ground" as it once accommodated a research station of the CPRI (Central Potato Research Institute): it has now been handed over to the Alain Duhangan project as a dumping site. It also houses a few thousand immigrant labourers for the project in ramshackle shacks; it was unbelievable to see this huge slum in such pristine natural surroundings. The rest of the potato ground is effectively an enormous latrine. The very existence of this place belies the voluminous EMPs (Environmental Management Plans) prepared by such projects and thoroughly exposes the state government's incapacity to ensure that these plans are implemented faithfully.

The stinking potato ground is located just below Sethan (2,650 metres), a collection of about 25 old, traditional houses. The road continues for another four kilometres beyond this point to Jabri; however, we had had enough of driving and wanted to get back on our legs and away from these symbols of economic development. So we left our vehicles here, shouldered our packs, and started climbing due northwards, through and past the potato ground and Sethan village, stepping gingerly around the piles of visiting cards left by the labourers, and soon left the stench and devastation behind us. Within half an hour or so we had left behind all signs of human presence, and after a gentle climb of another 90 minutes we came to a huge clearing in the forest—or thatch—called Sarotu Thatch, where the shepherds camp with their flocks in the summers (there were no shepherds when we reached Sarotu in September since by then they had moved further down to their winter grazing grounds). From here begins a much steeper climb northwards to a ridge called Kharmdiari (3,400 metres). The track dips sharply downwards at this point and winds its way almost back to the Alain River through dense forests of kharsu oak, levelling out about 50 metres above it on its left bank. The ubiquitous project road again appears on the left bank, leading to the forebay tank and the barrage, both clearly visible below us, where hectic construction activity was going on at full swing. The barrage is being constructed at a cleverly located place called Jabri: not only does it impound the waters of the Alain River, but it also traps the waters of another substantial stream, the Jabri Nullah, which debouches into the Alain just above the barrage. The combined waters

Gentle terrain above Chhikka

of these two streams shall flow into the forebay tank; below this, an underground tunnel coming from the east will convey the waters of the Duhangan stream (couple of kilometres to the east) into the Alain, and the combined waters of all three streams shall then be dropped a thousand metres to Prini to generate 190 MW of peaking power. The project is an engineering marvel; if only its environmental impacts could have been better addressed!

Thankfully, the project area and related activity ends at Jabri. Nature claims her own after this, and we reverted to the original trekking route, crossing the Jabri Nullah over a wooden bridge and proceeding on the left bank of the Alain. After a level walk of about a kilometre, one has to cross the Alain stream on to its right bank over a log bridge that had collapsed in the middle! As such, one has to descend first to the middle of the river, almost touching the foaming waters, and then ascend on the other side! Once on the right bank, it is a pleasant, almost level walk of about four kilometres to the first day's camping site at Chhikka (3,500 metres). This is a large, undulating meadow in a valley, just above the treeline, and the campsite is ideally located just below the point where a small stream cascades down from the ramparts to the west to join the Alain. A couple of Gujjar families were already camping here with their buffaloes, preparing to move down for the winters. We also saw a large number of stray cattle, mainly cows, roaming about, and were perplexed about their status till we learnt that it was customary for the villagers of Sethan and others to the south to leave their unproductive cows here in the summers, and collect them again before the onset of winter. We even met one energetic woman who had come to collect her cows! This simple expedient saves them the trouble and expense of feeding these cows till such time as they can conceive again. There is no or little risk involved in this practice: the cows cannot get lost because there is no place for them to go except this meadow/valley; there are no large predators here to endanger them except the occasional bear, which in any case would prefer a fat sheep to a cow any day. We reached Chhikka at about 5:00 pm—thick white clouds had started roiling up the valley from the south and we were soon shrouded in a blanket of white. High above us on either side, to the east and west, we could see white specks of sheep grazing on the slopes, still bathed in the light of the sun. Three mongrel dogs, no doubt camp followers of the neighbouring Gujjars, quickly came and introduced themselves to us, were rewarded with biscuits, and went off to perform their sentinel duties. We had had the foresight to carry some wood with us (no wood is available here because the place is above the treeline) and so lit a small campfire, had tea and dinner in this idyllic pastoral setting, and soon took to our tents for the night for it can suddenly become very cold at these heights.

Breakfast at Chhikka

The next day's campsite, a place called Ratan Thali, is about a six-hour trek so we left Chhikka at eight the next morning. One continues to go up the Alain stream on its right bank in a north-north-east alignment, climbing gently but steadily on a fairly well-defined track that hugs the river faithfully. The valley now starts narrowing: its walls to our left were quite precipitous and rocky, forcing us to stay close to the river itself; to the right (east), the walls were moderately inclined for most of the way, allowing for sloping pastures interspersed with scattered stands of white betula trees and huge clusters of dwarf rhododendron—ideal musk deer habitat. Occasionally the slopes ended in broad, sheer black rock faces, from which hung waterfalls akin to white ribbons. After about two hours the valley starts to open out, the gradient becomes easier, and soon we were into pasture territory again—a huge alpine meadow called Jaura Thatch with shin-high grasses, ferns, and flowers. It seems even the river loses its concentration in this idyllic spot for it begins to meander all over the pasture in small loops, as if reluctant to depart from here. We counted four Gaddi encampments and thousands of sheep. In fact, at one point we had to cross the stream over a typical log-and-stone bridge about 18 inches wide, but were held up for 15 minutes by a massive traffic jam! A few hundred sheep were making the crossing before us in single file, and pastoral philosophers that they are, they were in no particular hurry! Seeing this pasture and the one we had spent the previous night in, it was not difficult to understand why this route was so popular with the shepherds on their way to and from Spiti.

Giving a wide berth to the Gaddi encampments—for they were guarded by ferocious-looking dogs—we pressed on. The pasture soon reverted to valley shape, and after about an hour's trekking we abruptly debouched into a sandy plain about a kilometre long and half a kilometre wide, lying in a north-east–south-west alignment. The locals call this place "Balu ka Ghera" (literally, Ring of Sand). It is indeed a peculiar natural feature: a huge basin covered for the most part with sand and silt, through which the river meanders in half a dozen small channels. At its upper (north-east) end is a fairly large, circular lake ringed with sandy beaches, from which the place probably takes its name. The waters of the Alain, descending from the north-east, first collect in this basin before seeking an outlet to the south-west. The lake is usually full in the summer months when snowmelt is at its maximum; it was only half-full when we saw it. The guide informed us that this is prime black bear territory: just a couple of months back in June he had seen a mother bear frolicking in the lake with her two cubs. Thousands of sheep pass this way and the black bear have become used to preying on them from time to time, as if exacting a toll from those who cross their kingdom!

To the north-east, beyond the lake, Balu ka Ghera is sealed off by a 200-metre-high bluff, which is essentially a massive rockfall caused by centuries of erosion and glaciation of the towering mountains that can now be seen to the north and north-east. The Alain cascades down

Campsite at Ratan Thali this rockfall in a number of channels. We carefully skirted the lake and wearily clambered over the rockfall (it was now getting on to about four in the afternoon). Attaining its crest we found that we were on the ridgeline: straight ahead was an imposing mountain wall, veined with a number of glaciers and topped by an array of 5,700-metre peaks. Most of these peaks—Ratan Thali, Dharamsura, and Papsura—have never been scaled. The sun was blocked off by the high ramparts all around and the whole landscape was forbidding, almost primeval; we felt like we had no right to be there, that we were interlopers in this land of the wind, ice, and the black bear.

The crest or ridgeline that we had reached is actually a massive ledge that gradually merges into the flanks of the mountains towering above it to the north and north-east. A couple of glaciers almost reach down to this shelf; it is from these that the Alain takes birth. To the left of this ridge is a small grassy knoll dotted with huge boulders: this was our campsite for the night, Ratan Thali (3,900 metres)—supposedly named after an early explorer whose name was Ali Ratan. A well-marked nullah or watercourse enters the campsite from the north, its stream of crystal clear water flowing through the camp. We pitched our tents on one side of it and spent the rest of the evening gazing in awe at the many glaciers and snowfields dotting the mountain slopes to the north. Occasionally, huge white banks of clouds came rolling up the valley and within minutes the mountains would disappear completely; then, just as suddenly, the clouds would dissipate and the bright evening sunlight would reappear, pouring its warmth over the ridge and mountainsides. Later it became very cold and windy, and we took to our tents. During the night, on at least two occasions, I heard the muted thunder of big ice blocks breaking off from some glacier and falling into the valley far below.

The next day was the third and final day of the trek. Breaking camp at 8:00 am, we climbed along the nullah, heading north for 45 minutes or so. The nullah gradually opened out: the little stream itself veered to the right, and soon we could see the glacier from which it originated, high up on the mountain slopes to the north-east. We left the stream and stuck to the western end of this narrow valley, climbing steadily over rocks and moraine. After another 45 minutes we crested a rockfall and found ourselves on a saddle—this was Hamta Pass! We had ascended about 400 metres

Author and friends on the fog-shrouded Hamta Pass

View of Hamta River flowing down to join the Chandra   from our campsite. Spread out far below us was the savage grandeur and breathtaking beauty of the Hamta valley on the Lahaul side of the pass, with the Hamta River coursing down its middle like a thin, silvery braid; we were now standing on the ridgeline, or watershed, dividing the Lahaul and Kullu valleys, at an altitude of 4,227 metres.

It was quite windy at the pass and hence we did not tarry there for long. The descent on the Lahaul side is fairly steep but not difficult as the track is well defined and about a metre wide. We had to go down about 2,000 feet to reach the valley floor, and as we descended we realised that the valley of the Hamta was indeed quite wide, about 500–600 metres. Soon we could see the Hamta glacier to our right (or east), from which the stream originates. The Hamta is not a montane glacier (like the Chhatru glacier further down) but a riverine valley glacier, meaning that it lies in its own valley, which it has carved out over untold centuries. It took us about half an hour to reach the valley floor; when we did, we were pleasantly surprised to find a group of scientists from the Geological Survey of India (GSI) camping on the banks of the river. They informed us that they were from the glaciology division of the GSI and had been studying the Hamta glacier for the last 10 years! During this period the snout of the glacier had receded by almost a kilometre, and the discharge of the stream was also increasing each year. We walked upstream with them to the snout to see their measuring instruments, and were in fact quite surprised by the volume of water, which at this point was quite muddy from all the silt and detritus from the glacier. It was not an easy life for the GSI scientists here, who were based in Lucknow. They routinely spent five months each year at this camp—June to October; in fact, they were preparing to leave for the winter in a week or so. The team included two scientists, one cook, and some local labour; their facilities were very basic, communication to the outside world was through a two-way radio. It was a lonely existence and they were quite happy to see us. We spent about an hour with them before bidding them farewell.

We proceeded down the Hamta valley in a northerly direction, crossing the stream below the camp over a precarious iron bridge built by GSI, which is dismantled every winter when the scientists leave and reassembled the next summer when they return. It is a boon to the migratory shepherds and their flocks who would otherwise have to ford the river with all its attendant risks. The walk down the right bank of the Hamta was a uniquely pleasant experience: for almost five kilometres the terrain was a huge, gently sloping pasture. The river hugs the precipitous mountain slopes on its left bank while the right bank is rich grassland about two to three hundred metres wide, after which the mountainsides start rising again. Innumerable little streams of water trickle down these slopes and cross the pasture to join the Hamta, which gradually gains in size and volume. With the bright sun beating down on us it soon became very warm and we had to rapidly shed many layers of clothing. After about five kilometres the valley floor starts to descend at a more acute angle and the walls on either side start closing in. The grassland disappears, the terrain becomes rocky, and the sound of the Hamta becomes almost a roar, as if it realises that its journey's end is near. Finally, about eight kilometres after leaving the GSI camp we reached a ledge, falling away into a wide, massive valley meeting us at right angles and stretching in an East–West alignment. This was the valley of Chandra River, which originates about 80 km to the east of the Baralacha glacier, beyond the unbelievably enchanting and mysterious Chandratal lake.

The Hamta valley had become almost a gorge by now and the stream thundered 200 metres down the ledge to meet the Chandra; the track down is precipitous and dusty. After about 40 minutes we reached the valley floor which is more than a kilometre wide at this point. The Chandra flows along its farther, or northern side from east to west, about 50 metres wide. Above the river is the road from Keylong (the headquarters of Lahaul subdivision) that goes to Batal, Kunzum Pass, and then Kaza, the headquarters of Spiti. The valley floor is dotted with extensive grassy patches on which the shepherds obviously camp for the place is covered ankle-deep in sheep droppings. A number of small boys carrying huge sacks were busily collecting these droppings. On enquiring we learnt that they had been engaged by a local orchardist who used the droppings as manure—nothing is wasted here, where the cost of getting anything from the outside, even fertilizer, is prohibitive.

On reaching Chandra valley we turned left, or west, and followed the river downstream for a couple of kilometres on its left bank, crossed the river over an old iron bridge, and arrived at Chhatru—a staging point consisting of two shops and a rest house. High above Chhatru, on the towering mountain slopes to the north, one could see the outlines of a huge montane glacier: the Chhatru glacier. The melting waters from it join the Chandra in a roaring cascade a few hundred metres before the hamlet. The state govt has recently approved the construction of a huge hydel project at this point that shall capture the combined waters of the Chandra and Chhatru, and render the river dry for many kilometres downstream. The serenity of this valley shall disappear for ever in a few years. Nobody, of course, has bothered to study what impact the presence of thousands of labourers and an army of heavy machinery, burning lakhs of litres of fossil fuels, would have on the surrounding glaciers. We cast one last, wistful look at this untouched landscape, boarded our waiting vehicles at Chhatru, and settled our aching limbs for the four-hour drive back to Manali over the Rohtang Pass.

2006

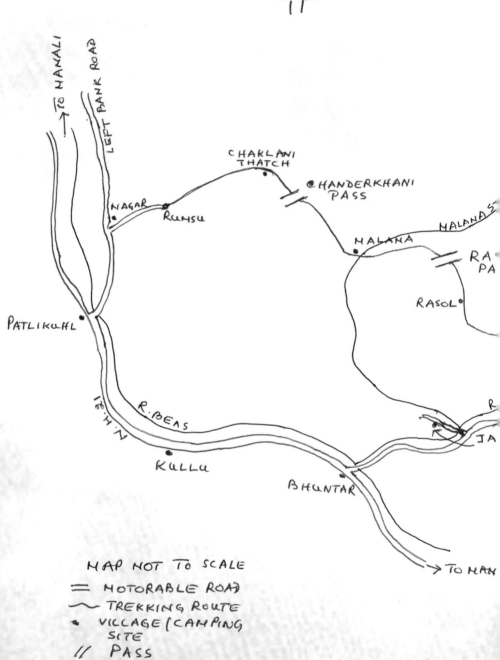

MAP NOT TO SCALE
= MOTORABLE ROAD
~ TREKKING ROUTE
• VILLAGE / CAMPING SITE
// PASS
~ RIVER / STREAM

Chandrakhani-Pass to Malana

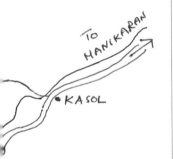

*M*alana, perhaps the most mysterious and internationally well-known village in the state, is situated in a gorge-like narrow valley between the upper Beas and Parbati valleys in Kullu district. The Malana gorge runs in an East–West alignment, guarded on the east by the 6,000-metre plus peaks of the Indrasen and Deo Tibba mountains, on the northern flank by the Chandrakhani Pass, and on the south by the Rasol Pass. The only access is from the west, upstream along the Malana stream from a place called Jari. A road has now reached Jari (thanks to the Malana-I Hydel project) and Malana is now just a strenuous three-hour walk from there. However, even five years ago Malana was completely landlocked and one had to trek for at least two days from any point to reach it. Its splendid isolation of centuries has spun many tales of the village and its mysterious residents, most of them equally hard to prove or disprove!

The most popular trekking route to Malana is from the north—from the tiny hamlet of Rumsu (six kilometres above Naggar) in the Beas valley, situated at 1,800 metres. Naggar is located on the road on the left bank of the river Beas, about 24 km downstream of Manali. It is famous for two institutions—the

Naggar castle and the Roerich Museum. Naggar castle served as the original seat of power of the rulers of Kullu before they shifted to Kullu town. It is a wood-and-stone structure of charming design and commands a spectacular view of the Beas, the orchards on either side, and the majestic mountain ranges to the north. The rooms of the castle are built around a central courtyard, which itself contains an exquisitely carved temple where the kings of Kullu used to worship. After the rulers shifted to Kullu in the nineteenth century the castle became the official residence of the British resident here, and now belongs to the Himachal government—it is now one of the heritage hotels of the Himachal Pradesh Tourism Development Corporation (HPTDC). The second item of note in Naggar, the Roerich Museum, is housed in a sprawling estate of the same name, commemorating the mountainscapes of this Russian artist whose love of the mountains inspired his life and art. One cannot pass through Naggar and not visit these places.

The trek starts at Rumsu, a tiny hamlet located six kilometres above Naggar on a steep *katcha* road that snakes its way through cultivated fields and orchards. One has to climb, steeply at first and then more gently, in a southerly direction through dense forests of deodar, spruce, and horse chestnut for three hours, crossing Stellag Thatch and Dhan Karari Thatch. A thatch is essentially a clearing in a forest that usually has a water source and where shepherds camp. From the latter one can get a panoramic, wide-angled view of the majestic Pir Panjal range towards the north; can clearly spot the peaks of Friendship mountain, Hanuman Tibba, Shittidhar, and Patalsu; and guess at the location of the Kalihani Pass, beyond which lies the even more mysterious and forbidding valley of Bara Bhangal. It was June when we made the trek and all the ranges were covered with a thick layer of snow. However, half way up the snowline we could distinctly see a brownish, smudged line running across the entire range: a layer of dust and soot deposited on the snow up to a height of about 3,000 metres, the result of dust storms and pollution in the Beas valley, contributed in no small measure by the tens of thousands of vehicles that come to the valley every summer. This was another indication, if one were needed, that tourism in Himachal

the way it is being practised is not environmentally sustainable. It was a
disturbing sight to say the least. Straight ahead, due north and across the
Beas, one could see the shining penstock pipes of the Baragram micro-
hydel project commissioned recently. At Dhan Karari the track swerves
eastwards following the ridgeline, and after two hours one reaches
the campsite—another huge thatch called Chaklani (3,300 metres),
surrounded by dwarf rhododendron that were in full bloom, ringing
the pasture in pink and mauve. This is an ideal camping site for the
first day: good glacial meltwater is available, and the Chandrakhani Pass
is clearly visible about two kilometres away, one of the most beautiful
passes I have seen in Himachal. Its massive flanks are gently inclined
(unlike the barren, rocky approaches of other passes), and are almost
completely carpeted with spruce, birch, and betula (*bhojpatra*) till about
200 metres below the saddle, from where the snow takes over. One

Rhododendrons framing the Chandrakhani Pass

should bring one's own tent and provisions for camping here, though during the main trekking season some intrepid entrepreneurs do set up their tents here, offering night stay, food, and sleeping bags for a reasonable payment. These are encroachments on forest land, but since they provide an essential service and promote tourism, the forest officials look the other way as long as no permanent structures are set up and no poaching takes place. (Incidentally, Chaklani is prime musk deer habitat).

Breaking camp at 7:00 am the next day, it took us about two hours to reach the pass: the climb is not steep since one has to make diagonal traverses on the flanks, but the snow was about four feet deep, the cold night had frozen it to ice, and each step had to be carefully placed. It was mid-June when we made this trek and the snows on the pass usually melt by this time. But this year Kullu valley had had an extended winter and snowfall had taken place as late as end-May, and so the pass was covered with more ice than we had anticipated. For this reason we were unable to take mules along with us. We were not the first ones to make the trek this year, however. This route is traditionally thrown open after the winters every year by a *jatha* or group of devotees carrying their local *devtas* or gods, singing, dancing, and chanting all the way to Malana. It must be an awe-inspiring sight to witness this sturdy and courageous display of faith: we learnt that this group had crossed the pass some two weeks earlier, albeit with great difficulty. We were somewhat relieved at this piece of information since at first sight it did appear, at least from this distance, that perhaps there was too much ice on the pass for it to be crossed. The saddle on top is about 50 metres wide and dotted with cairns. This, however, is not the pass and one should not cross from this point for it soon ends in an un-negotiable precipice. One should continue to traverse in an easterly direction for another 100 metres or so till a small cleft in the ridge on one's right—this is the actual pass. Local myth has it that Jamadagni Rishi, also known as Jamlu devta—the *devta* or deity of Malana—once came to this place, clutching in his fists a number of smaller gods. He was very angry

for some reason and scattered these smaller gods: the wind carried them to various parts of Kullu district where each is revered as the local deity of the village he happened to land in. But Jamlu devta still considers them his inferiors and thus, to this day, he does not join the Kullu Dussehra (which is attended by dozens of the "smaller" gods), and prefers to watch the festivities from the distant heights of Bijli Mahadev! He is a difficult god and a bit of a renegade. When a police party first attempted to raid Malana village many years ago on account of its cannabis cultivation, Jamlu devta did not allow them to enter the village for many days! The peaks that appear to the east now are even more spectacular: Indrasen, Deo Tibba, and the Malana glacier, below which is spread out the vast expanse of Nagroni pasture, a favourite camping ground for foreign trekkers, half a day's trek from the pass.

Malana village. The Chandrakhani Pass is in the cleft in the high range behind it

The descent on the southern face is unremittingly precipitous for 6,000 feet, along a watercourse, till one reaches the track leading to the village of Malana, situated about 200 metres above the Malana stream that originates from the glacier visible from the pass. It's a large village of about 150 houses, totally landlocked till about six years ago. It does not welcome outsiders and fiercely guards its traditions and distinct culture. Its residents are thought to be descendants of Greek soldiers: local history has it that one detachment of Alexander's army, exhausted from the years of unremitting warfare, hid in this valley when Alexander crossed the Indus, and settled here instead of going back to Greece. The soldiers intermarried with the locals (one occasionally comes across a striking face with uncharacteristic aquiline features, blue eyes, or blonde hair) and developed an isolated synthesis of the two cultures. Malana is reported to be the oldest democracy in the world, has its own parliament with upper and lower houses, and still has its own laws and system of justice administration. Monetary fines are imposed on villagers who break these laws; all disputes are resolved by its parliament and anyone who approaches the district administration is fined! Till a few years ago even a government official who wished to visit the village had to obtain prior approval of the *devta* or local deity. Alcohol is not permitted in the panchayat, and marriage with an outsider is banned, although a few outside marriages have now begun to take place. Desperate as it is to cling to its splendid, isolated past, Malana is now changing, thanks primarily to the hydel project which has come up at Jari on the Malana stream. About three hours downstream, the attendant induction of thousands of outside labourers and crores of project funds has created a slew of economic opportunities, as also the ubiquitous road.

Malana's claim to fame, however, is its cannabis. Though its cultivation is illegal, the villagers do so on hundreds of acres, till now secure in their inaccessibility. "Malana Cream" is reported to be the best hash in the world and goes by many other interesting names: AK-47, Russian Mist, Space Ball, Manali Cream, etc. The drug sells for about 25,000 rupees per kg at Malana, and its international price, we were told, was between $22,000 and $25,000. Naturally, therefore, the village draws hundreds of foreigners every year who stay in the village for months, living the classic life of the lotus eaters. The whole economy of the village/panchayat now depends on cannabis. The state government, however, appears to have a very ambivalent approach to the whole issue. At one level, resolutions have been passed in the state legislature demanding that the cultivation of the plant in this area be declared legal since the people have no other economic activity, and the fibres of the hemp plant are also used by the local populace for making bags, ropes, shoes, and floor coverings; the state government has forwarded these resolutions to the central government. At another level, however, the agencies of the state, since 2002, have started raiding the valley regularly each year, destroying hundreds of acres of the plant. We saw the result of these raids ourselves in 2005: cannabis is no longer grown in the fields of the village, which have been given over to wheat, rajmash, and sundry vegetables. But move away from the village into the thick forests on the higher mountain slopes and cannabis is grown in abundance—the activity has simply been shifted

A (typical) dogri at Malana where we spent the night

to areas more difficult for the police to locate. Given the difficult terrain and their own level of physical fitness, this is a battle the enforcement agencies simply cannot win, notwithstanding the statistics churned out by them in press conferences.

The residents of Malana have a traditional distrust for government officials and hence we decided not to spend the night in the village, even though we were completely exhausted by the descent from Chandrakhani Pass. We crossed the Malana stream and proceeded south for another kilometre to Nagrain: here the cultivated fields disappear and the forest reappears. Only a few scattered *dogris* exist here—wood-and-slate double-storeyed huts that are used by their owners off and on for forays into the forests for dubious purposes such as poaching, felling trees, and growing cannabis. We stayed in one of these *dogris* for the night, courtesy the forest guard whose khaki-clad request to the owner could not be refused!

The climb to Rasol Pass starts from Nagrain itself. In fact, the pass is clearly visible from here as a sharp cleft in the densely wooded ridge straight ahead, about 1,000 metres higher up. The ascent is along a watercourse for the first 200 metres, followed by thick, steep forests for another 500 metres. We met an old lady in these forests, looking for her two cows who had wandered into the jungle the previous evening. She had found one of them dead, killed and partly eaten by a black bear. She informed us that a female bear with two cubs had wandered into these forests, and was fully expecting the second cow to have been killed too. Bears are generally vegetarian but will not pass up the opportunity of some meat, and regularly kill cattle and sheep in these mountains if they are left unguarded. A bear with cubs would require a lot of food and would also be extremely dangerous. We bunched up after this, talking in loud voices so as to scare the animal away if it happened to be in the vicinity. After about an hour we emerged from the forests onto a gently inclining and beautiful pasture that wound its way to the cleft that was the Rasol Pass (3,200 metres). We saw that the fields had been cleared here and planted with cannabis! The hidden moral of the story was quite clear to us, even if the government is oblivious to it: unless the people here are offered an alternative economic activity, they would continue to cultivate this crop, no matter how many legions are sent up. The folks of Malana do not do this because it is easy money. In fact, it is far from easy—developing a field at these heights, planting, protecting, and harvesting it in the face of hostile and life-threatening weather conditions—all this is back-breaking and dangerous work. With one-tenth the sheer physical effort put in here one could cultivate ten times this area in the plains. But the plains and their controlled conditions are not available to the citizens of Malana, and they really have no choice. The sooner the state and central governments realise this and come up with a workable alternative that respects the basic laws of economics, the sooner they shall be able to eradicate this drug problem; knee-jerk, goose-stepping solutions cannot work in these extreme terrains.

The view from here was again panoramic, especially to the north-east where the massive Malana glacier was now clearly visible, and also the vast expanse of Nagroni Thatch: even from this distance we could see the *dogris* on the pasture where the foreign trekkers camp for days together. The full extent of the Malana valley could be seen, stretching another 10 km or so beyond the village to the snout of the glacier. Somewhere on this stretch is the site for the proposed second stage of the Malana hydel project, which shall ensure that the cultural and historical uniqueness of this valley is erased for ever. The north is dominated by the Chandrakhani Pass, which we had negotiated the previous day. To the south one could see the high ridges of the Kanawar Sanctuary in the distance, and a slender thread of silver, which was the Parbati River, was visible about 4,000 feet below us. Along its banks, on the other side, one could just discern a few rooftops of Kasol village, the roadhead.

The descent from Rasol Pass is as precipitous as that from Chandrakhani and just as exhausting. Almost half way down is the village of Rasol, a dirty cluster of about 50 houses: its main, cobbled street also doubles as the central drain, and since it was raining when we reached there, we splashed our way through the village, surprised that such a small place could generate so much garbage!

A bird's-eye view of Kanawar Sanctuary from Rasol Pass

The village elders met us and demanded that the local primary school be upgraded to a middle school as the nearest middle school was at Kasol, more than eight kilometres away. And thereby, we discovered, hung a sordid political tale! It appears that during the last elections to the state assembly, the Congress candidate had promised this upgradation. Unfortunately for the simple citizens of Rasol this chap lost the elections, which was won by the BJP candidate—the Congress aspirant received only eight votes from this village! Even worse, the government in the state was formed by the Congress. So now the burghers of Rasol faced a typical Indian conundrum: their MLA was of no use because he belonged to the Opposition, and the defeated Congress heavyweight would not help them since he was still sulking at having received only eight votes from the village! We promised to convey their demand to the government and left them doing their calculations for the next elections!

It is eight kilometres from Rasol to the roadhead village of Kasol: a constant descent, but not as steep as before; a track emerges after about five kilometres and the going becomes much easier. After about six more kilometres one reaches Chalal, a sprawling hamlet of about 40 houses on the right bank of the Parbati. Every second house here is either a guest house or a restaurant or a pool parlour! This is the base for excursions into the Malana valley and caters to the foreign visitors, and consequently does very well economically. The track from here to Kasol, which is on the other (left) bank of the river, is a delightful sylvan walk: almost level, it hugs the riverbank and winds its way through the thick foliage that comes right to the river's edge on either bank, improved and set with stones by the forest department. The thundering, foaming Parbati River roars by on the right, not yet tamed by the forces of development. The ambience is absolutely mesmerising and one could sit for hours on a huge boulder, watching the waters that change their shape every second and yet have been the same for thousands of years. There is no better example than a mountain river of the ever-changing permanence of nature. All too soon the walk is over: the track turns to the right and crosses the river on a bridge made of iron ropes and wooden planks, about 50 metres long. The first building on the left bank is the forest rest house, a big wooden cottage of three rooms that is almost a hundred years old. It has been renovated recently and is very well appointed, with tiled bathrooms, geysers, and modern furniture. It is set in the middle of lush lawns and flower beds, and looks eastwards towards the massive mountain ranges of Pin Parbat from where the river is born. It is an ideal place to stay after the exhausting three days of the trek. Reservations can be made with the DFO (Divisional Forest Officer) Parbati, whose office is at Bhuntar. Next to the forest rest house is a guest house of the Himachal Pradesh Tourism Development Corporation, which has six rooms and is equally comfortable. Some way beyond these rest houses is Kasol proper—grown into a small township now from the village that it was barely 10 years ago.

Kasol is a mini Manali, consisting almost entirely of hotels, restaurants, internet cafes, pool parlours, gift shops, bakeries, pizzerias, etc. The cuisines on offer in the eateries is truly international—German, Italian, Chinese, Continental, Israeli—and so too are the crowds. The town caters almost exclusively to foreigners and is the centre of all drug-related activities in the Kullu valley. It sits at a crossroad: to the north is Malana valley, and to the east is the even more remote Parbati valley—cannabis and other narcotic plants are grown in abundance in places like Pulga and Kheer Ganga where the police are yet to reach. Kasol is a haven for young foreign druggies, some of whom have even begun marrying the local girls and are settling down to a permanent life of drug-induced oblivion. Of late other nationalities are being edged out by the Israelis, who come here in large numbers after doing their compulsory draft in the Israeli army, their pockets full of back wages. They are low-budget, aggressive, and prepared to stay on for long times. In fact, so concerned is the Israeli government that it has now established a couple of counselling centres in Kullu to try and wean the youngsters

Parbati River in all its splendour at Kasol

back to the more traditional ways of Jewish life. We learnt that even a synagogue was due to come up here. During the full-moon period secret parties are held deep inside the forests around Kasol, complete with amplified music systems, food, and all kinds of drugs. People of all nationalities congregate at these parties. For some reason the local police feel these gatherings are illegal, try to find out their venue, hardly ever succeed, and so the cat and mouse game goes on. However, there is no doubt that the drug-centric activities and visitors in Kasol do pose a serious social and legal problem for the administration. The foreign tourists may be here just to "chill out" for a few days, but in order to service them a whole industry has been established, link by link, and its tentacles are now spreading far beyond Kasol or even Himachal. The Centre is becoming increasingly concerned about the activities here as it now suspects that some of the drug moneys generated is being used to fund terrorism related activities both within and outside the country. The lure of easy profits shall soon attract the purveyors of other related criminal activities with predictable consequences for this idyllic valley.

From Kasol it is one hour by road to Bhuntar on the main Mandi–Manali national highway. Bhuntar is also the point where the river Parbati joins the Beas. We had come half circle, in a way—starting from the Beas near Naggar, we crossed two valleys and joined the Beas again 50 km downstream, having completed what is now coming to be known as the "cannabis circuit"!

2005

TREKS IN
LAHAUL AND SPITI
DISTRICT

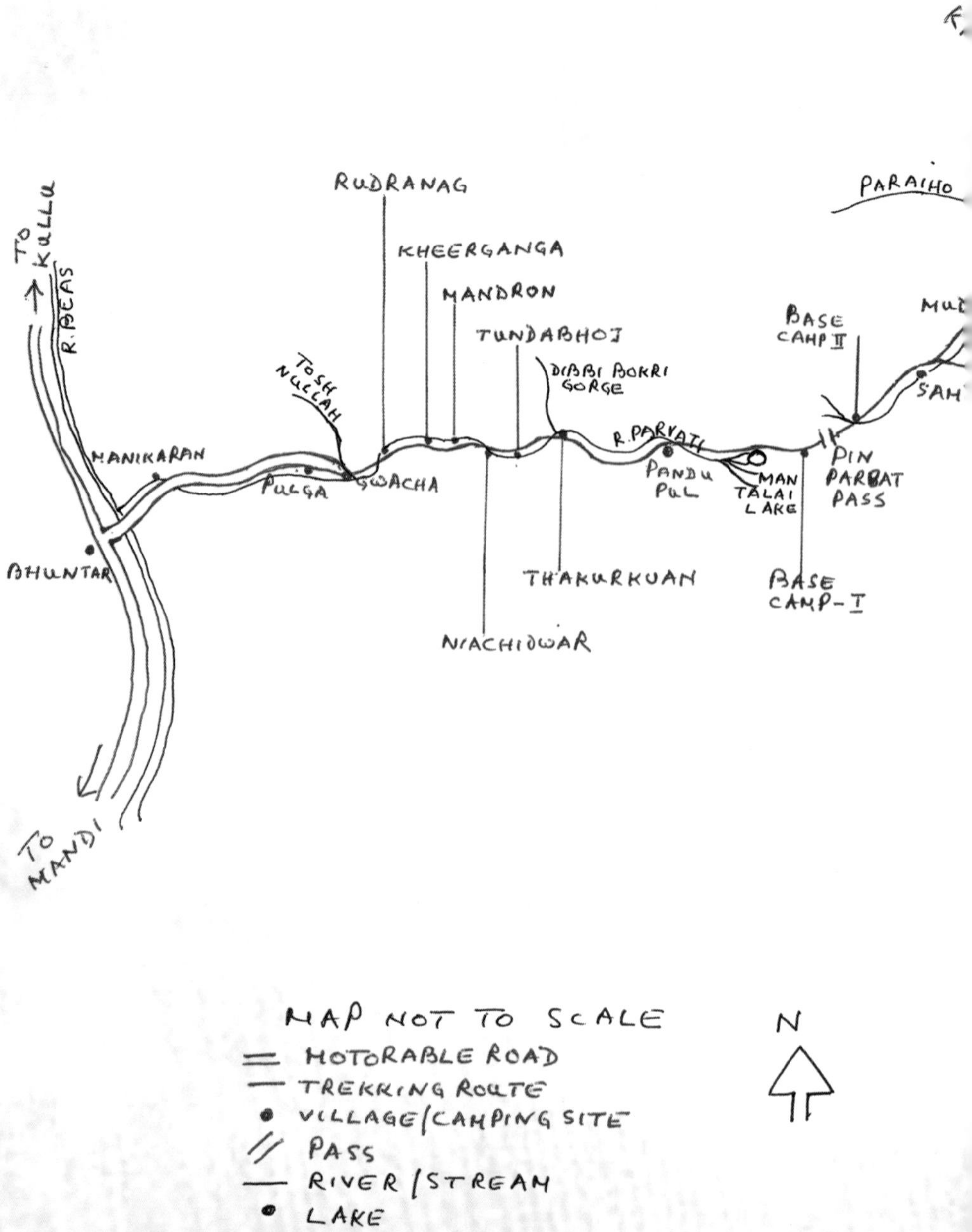

RUDRANAG

KHEERGANGA

MANDRON

TUNDABHOJ

PARAIHO

TOSH
NULLAH

DIBBI BOKRI
GORGE

BASE
CAMP II

MUL

TO KULLU

R. BEAS

MANIKARAN

PULGA

SWACHA

R. PARVATI

PANDU
PUL

MAN
TALAI
LAKE

PIN
PARBAT
PASS

SAH

BHUNTAR

THAKURKUAN

BASE
CAMP-I

NIACHIDWAR

TO MANDI

MAP NOT TO SCALE

MOTORABLE ROAD
TREKKING ROUTE
VILLAGE/CAMPING SITE
PASS
RIVER/STREAM
LAKE

N

Pin-Parbat
A TALE OF TWO
RIVERS AND A PASS

The Pin Parbat Pass, at 18,000 feet, straddles two districts—on its southern side is Kullu and the northern aspect is in Lahaul-Spiti. But it does more than just separate two districts; it also separates two absolutely different climatic zones and ecosystems, and acts as a watershed for two enchanting rivers: the Parbati draining the southern side and the Pin the terrain on the north. South of the pass on the Kullu side, the Parbati basin is covered with dense and varied vegetation, beautiful forests giving way to magnificent alpine pastures on the heights. However, the valley of the Pin River to the north is a cold desert and absolutely devoid of any vegetation, a frozen canvas of sculpted rocks and lonely peaks bathed in the most amazing colours conceivable. One can well imagine, therefore, that though the trek to the Pin Parbat Pass can be arduous and sometimes dangerous, the rewards which await the intrepid trekker who attempts the trek make the effort and the toil more than worthwhile. About 100 persons make this trek in a year, a large number of them foreigners. However, this trek should not be taken lightly: one should be well-equipped with provisions for about eight days, a good guide is absolutely essential, and one should not attempt to do a solo trek (quite often foreign trekkers, unaware that the Himalayas have more surprises than do the Alps or the Rockies, venture out alone and are never seen or heard of again). One needs to be in excellent physical condition for these heights; carrying of basic mountain gear such as ice axes and ropes is also advisable as there are gorges and glaciers to be negotiated. Essential medical provisions are a must and one needs to constantly keep an eye out for symptoms of mountain/altitude sickness—more than one trekker has lost his life simply because these symptoms could not be recognised in time.

The trek can be attempted from either flank, but the route from the Kullu side is comparatively easier and is the more preferred option. This was the route we took. Coming via the national highway (Mandi–Kullu) one crosses the Beas at Bhuntar, the place of its confluence with the Parbati, drives up the Parbati valley on the left bank of the river, past Manikaran and its huge gurdwara and hot springs, to a small hamlet called Gwacha where the road ends. (Much of Manikaran, the gurdwara, and its hot springs were washed away by massive floods about five years after we undertook this trek). Gwacha is located at a point where a sizeable stream called the Tosh Nullah meets the Parbati. It is the base camp for the trek and boasts of a two-room rest house of the HPSEB (Himachal Pradesh State Electricity Board) where one can spend the night before beginning the trek the next day.

The first day requires one to cover about 18 km and to ascend gently to a height of 3,300 metres, and is therefore good acclimatisation for the more arduous climbs to come. Initially moving up on the left bank of the Tosh, one turns into the Parbati valley on its right bank, and passes through the sleepy and unique village of Pulga after about a kilometre. Pulga, with its 100 odd houses, is the gateway to the Parbati valley, and what makes it unique is the presence of foreigners in large numbers. Some of the best hashish in the world is grown in the area and Pulga, much to the embarrassment of the local administration, has become the centre of the trade here. This explains the presence of not only the itinerant foreigners but also the dozens who have more or less settled here. The latter are so enchanted by the idyllic beauty of the place and easy availability of the drug that they have consciously opted to live the lives of the classic lotus eaters: it is reported that a few have even married local girls and now own lands and property here! There is even a bakery in the village that makes French bread and pizzas!

From Pulga one ascends through gently sloping cultivated fields to Nagthan, the last village in the valley, comprising about 200 souls. About two kilometres beyond Nagthan one reaches Rudra-Nag, a place consisting of one dilapidated temple of indeterminate age and a waterfall in the shape of a serpent with its hood extended, a feature from which the place obviously gets its name. Local legend has it that the god Shiva once told his sons Ganesh and Kartik to travel around the world and meditate as that was the only way to attain enlightenment. While Kartik took his father at his word and set out to circumnavigate the globe, Ganesh walked in a circle around Shiva and, claiming that his father was his world, sat down there itself and began meditating. It then started raining; a huge serpent appeared from the forests and spread its massive hood over Ganesh to shield him from the rain. This is how local folklore explains the shape of the waterfall and the name of this place. Indeed, the Parbati valley, though practically uninhabited, is rich in such myths (as we were to discover later), and this adds an enchanting flavour to the treks. At Rudra-Nag, we crossed over to the left bank of the Parbati on a wooden bridge, and immediately began a very steep climb through thick forests of fir and spruce. After about 40 minutes, we entered an unusual forest of walnut, the green of the fir and spruce giving way to a ghostly pale white. This must surely be one of the last walnut groves in the state as the species is becoming rare in the wild, prompting the state government to impose a complete ban on its felling. Without any warning we broke out of this silent grove and came face to face with a signboard, on which was crudely lettered: SHARMA RESTAURANT! This was Ishidwara and the enterprising Mr Sharma ran a dhaba (a simple, rustic eatery) here, catering to the few trekkers, the Gujjars, and the Gaddis—the true and itinerant residents of Parbati valley. This is something I have always encountered, and marvelled at, on my numerous treks in all parts of the state: the intrepid spirit of commerce that makes people like Sharmaji set up shop in the remotest,

loneliest, quite often inhospitable places imaginable, providing a service whose value cannot be computed in cash. Market forces do not just operate in the metropolises of our country; they are also active in the little heard of valleys and mountains, keeping alive in the process a way of life that has subsisted for thousands of years. Establishments like Sharmaji's are also important clearing houses for local information, which can sometimes be vital for those who travel on these isolated routes. Information, for instance, about the weather up ahead, the state of the track and the bridges on it, the various parties en route, possible accidents, and so on.

We were almost in the middle of September—Sharmaji informed us that he would be packing and closing up his shop in another week, and heading back to his village in Kangra district as winter would be setting in pretty soon; he would return in April/May the next year. Quite often, his little structure would have been demolished by bears during the winter sojourn. However, since it was made entirely of locally obtained wood, it would not take Sharmaji long to be back in business, with the local forest guard obligingly looking the other way! Wishing him well, and after imbibing a couple of strong cups of tea, we proceeded onwards. After about another 10 km we came to the most prominent point on this part of the trek—Kheer Ganga or the "River of Milk". Situated at a height of 2,900 metres on a pasture-like ridge jutting above the forests, Kheer Ganga consists of about a dozen rough wooden structures functioning as hotels and eating houses, along with a temple. What makes this place relatively famous and gives it its peculiar name, however, is a tank next to the temple, filled with hot water welling up from underground sulphur springs. This water has left white rings or bands all around the tank, no doubt caused by residual minerals in the sulphur-heated water, but this is enough to bestow on the place a religious significance and give it its name. During the season, and on good days, about a hundred people trek up to this place from Pulga each day to take a dip in this sacred tank. The dhabas do a flourishing business, and the fare they offer is surprisingly wide and satisfying: one can order Chinese food,

pasta, and pizzas in addition to the normal Indian stuff! We took a refreshing dip in the pool, gorged ourselves on the last decent meal we were going to have for the next week, and even took a siesta! After this point we would really be on our own, barring the occasional Gujjar or Gaddi.

Leaving Kheer Ganga at 4:00 pm, we trekked through relatively sparse forests, crossing Dhara Thatch and Nihara Thatch. A "thatch" is a big clearing in a forest where Gujjars, nomadic cattle (mainly buffalo) herders who are usually Muslim, or Gaddis, shepherds, usually camp, sometimes for months. The thatches we crossed were deserted since it was late in the year and most Gujjars had already descended to lower altitudes. The Gujjar's is an interesting lifestyle: they are essentially nomadic, or transhumant, peoples; they don't usually own any lands

Dense forests above Kheer Ganga

but have grazing and camping rights in pastures and forests, even in the remotest corners, which have been subsisting for generations. Neither geographical nor political boundaries matter for them and they travel freely from state to state. For example, the Gujjars in Himachal spend their winters in the adjacent areas of Punjab or Haryana, and some even have rights in Uttaranchal. They are a closed community by the very nature of their existence. Though leading a life devoid of comforts as we know them and lacking in liquidity, they possess a lot of wealth on the hoof. A typical family would have about 20 or 25 milch buffalo of superior breed, each worth anything between rupees twenty five or thirty thousand. The community also plays an important role in the economy of rural Himachal, providing milk, *khoya*, and paneer to the rural markets, especially in the more remote areas that are not otherwise connected to the usual marketing or distribution channels. They are an extremely tough breed of people—the average Gujjar would think nothing of carrying 30 or 40 kilos of milk or milk products 10 km to the nearest market, and return to his thatch by the evening! They have classical Aryan features and their women are handsome and stately. It is an amazing community, but one which is destined to die out in a couple of generations under the onslaught of internal and external pressures. On the outside, the construction of roads, better networking of distribution/marketing channels, reduced access to forests and pastures because of conservation and environmental imperatives—all these are gradually making the Gujjar redundant in a modern market economy system, and taking away from him the vast spaces and unencumbered solitudes that provide oxygen to his lifeblood. From within too the signs of decay are evident—the Gujjar youth of today are gradually becoming aware, they want to go to school, they want a settled existence, they would prefer professions that are not so arduous and where the returns are more. We may not see this "noble savage" for very much longer.

We reached Mandron on the left bank of the Parbati at about 6:00 pm amidst a light mizzle. This was to be our first night's camping site. Mandron may have a name, but little else. All it had was the encampment of one Gujjar, Lal Hussain. He insisted that we dine with him and plied us with glasses of rich, creamy milk. He owned about 20 buffalo, and since he was so far away from the nearest market of any consequence (Manikaran is 35 km away) he converted his milk into *khoya*, sending 30 to 40 kg of it down to Manikaran every third day. We estimated that he would be selling at least 12,000 to 15,000 rupees worth of *khoya* each month, and tried our best to pry out of him what he did with this money or where he kept it, but got nothing out of Lal Hussain except another glass of milk. We went to sleep that night in our tents enshrouded in the mist and drizzle, dreaming of Lal Hussain's buried treasure trove!

The drizzle had given way to bright sunshine by the next morning. After breakfasting with Lal Hussain and his many wives, we bade him adieu and pressed up the Parbati valley, which at this point was 250 metres wide with the river flowing quietly a hundred feet below. I am always amazed at how even the most remote places that have never had any habitation have nonetheless acquired names. And so we trekked past Tanak Vihar (distinguished by a soaring waterfall on the other side of the river—a great photo op. that we did not miss) and Tunda Bhoj. Now, "bhoj" refers to the *bhojpatra* tree, which abounds in this part of the valley, and "tunda" means a cripple: right next to the track stands a huge *bhojpatra* tree with its top blown off, most probably by lightning, and that's how the place got its name. We then arrived at Niachidwar, about 10 km from Mandron, where we were required to cross over to the right bank of the river. Easier said than done!

The left bank of the Parbati (where we were) is precipitous at this spot, and the right bank slopes down to the river in gently inclined shelves. The width is about 20 metres and the river itself thunders through this near-gorge with some force. Spanning the river was a wire rope on which was suspended a metal basket just big enough to contain a big bag of food grains or a small contorted human being: the process of crossing the river comprised of getting into this basket and hauling oneself across by pulling on a rope attached to the basket. A primitive system but an effective one nonetheless, requiring no maintenance and totally self-sufficient. We were to discover in the coming days that this

was the standard method of crossing gorges in these parts. All this equipment had been installed by the state electricity board, not out of any altruistic motives however, but because for some years now it has been investigating the hydel potential of the Parbati valley (about which more shall be related later on).

We made the crossing, the most disturbing part of it being the structural dynamics of the wire rope on which was suspended the basket; something which I, being from an arts background, did not realise till it was too late! Now, this rope naturally sags in the middle: when one pushes off from one bank, therefore, one is initially on a downward slope and makes good speed till the lowest part of the sag is reached, and then stops completely running out of momentum. At this point one starts pulling on the second rope (or screams at the people on the other bank to do so), hauling one up to the other bank. However, for about 40 or 50 seconds one is hanging completely stationary, suspended over the deepest part of the river! And it is usually at this point that the basket is the most unstable and begins a gentle swaying motion! Believe me, the first time one is completely disoriented, the heart-thumping fear further compounded by the deafening roar of the river; even the strongest man, when he reaches the other side, has a noticeable quiver in his legs.

We witnessed a remarkable spectacle on the other side. A group of shepherds had arrived from the opposite direction and had to cross the river at the same point on their way down to Manikaran. The sheep were put in the basket two at a time and hauled across, but their horses (about six in number) were too big to effect a passage in the basket. A long, thick rope was tied firmly around the neck of a horse; one person crossed over to the other side (via the wire suspended basket) with one end of the rope and took up position about 50 yards downstream of the crossing point. The other end of the rope was held by the persons on the right bank with the horse now tied from both sides and in the middle of the rope. The shepherds on the near bank then drove the horse into the swiftly flowing river and within seconds the poor creature was swept off his feet by the torrent, completely disappearing under the

waters. The shepherds on both banks hauled mightily on the rope and, after a few agonising seconds, the horse reappeared as a black speck on the foaming waters, still being swept downstream but with his velocity arrested by the rope. The chaps on the right bank now eased the hauling on the rope while still maintaining a firm grip on it. The persons on the left bank, conversely, redoubled their efforts; gradually the horse started moving towards the left bank in an oblique line, adding his own massive strength to that of his straining masters. Within a minute or less the horse scrambled on to the left bank about a 100 metres below his original starting point, none the worse for his dunking. All the horses had crossed over in about an hour's time in the same manner. It was an absolutely amazing performance, and one which reinforced in our minds the rugged, risky quality of these nomads' existence, as well as the manner in which their lives are completely attuned to the rhythms of nature. These children of this remote land never fight nature for that

A horse fording the Parbati River

would be futile; instead, they use the infinite strength of nature to serve their purposes. This was symbolically conveyed to each one of us by the manner in which the shepherds used the force of the river itself to carry the horses downstream and to the opposite bank, guided only by a rope held in their hands.

From Niachidwar it is an almost level walk of about six kilometres to Thakur Kuan, where one crosses back to the left bank of the Parbati via a similar wire-and-pulley bridge. The valley begins to widen out at this point. There is an abandoned and vandalised inspection hut of the HPSEB here, constructed as part of the survey-and-investigation exercise of the valley. We found that the floorboards had been ripped out (no doubt to burn on some harsh winter night by shepherds), and there were signs indicating that people camp here regularly. Looking straight ahead from the hut in a north-east direction, upstream, a deep gorge meets the Parbati on its right side, contributing a massive volume of water to the main river. This is the forbidding-sounding Dibbi Bokri gorge, which has an interesting tale of wickedness attached to it. It is related in these parts that many years ago a Britisher came prospecting in these mountains and discovered a rich vein of precious stones in the Dibbi Bokri gorge. He started mining it with the help of two Gurkha labourers and soon collected a veritable hoard. One day, after a few months of mining, as usual he let the Gurkhas down into the gorge on a thick rope, playing out the rope from the lip of the canyon, which can be as deep as a thousand feet at some points. When the poor Gurkhas were halfway down he cut the rope, sending them plummeting to their deaths; their bodies, obviously, were never found. Having eliminated the only other people who knew the location of the mother lode, the Britisher gathered his precious hoard and disappeared. No one has ever seen him again. Some shepherds have occasionally tried to look for his mine but without any success, for the gorge is so deep and dangerous that any sustained effort is impossible.

The Dibbi Bokri gorge meets the Parbati about one kilometre upstream of the HPSEB inspection hut. The valley here is almost a kilometre wide with the river flowing down its right side—the left bank consisting of sloping pastures and the right bank bounded by precipitous escarpments. This is the site for one of the most hare-brained schemes devised by the HPSEB. The board has proposed to build a huge dam at a place about half a kilometre below the point at which the Dibbi Bokri stream meets the Parbati. The proposal (officially known as stage-I of the Parbati Hydel Project) involves impounding the waters of the river at this site and then taking them through an underground tunnel to Pulga, where a powerhouse would be located to generate 800 MW of power. The project would be an environmental disaster of huge proportions. A road capable of carrying heavy machinery would have to be constructed all the way from Pulga to Dibbi Bokri: the havoc and destruction this would cause to the forests and pastures cannot even be imagined. A huge reservoir, almost a kilometre wide and stretching for 10 km all the way upstream to Pandupul, would be created, blocking off for ever the migratory routes of the wildlife to the lower elevations of the valley. This will have genetically disastrous consequences for their breeding cycles, and indeed put a big question mark on their very survival if they are not able to move down in the winters. Not surprisingly, the HPSEB has not carried out any environmental impact assessment before framing this proposal. The technical parameters of this project are also highly suspect since the reservoir would be frozen for at least five months in the year! Fortunately though, the scheme has not yet received environmental clearance from the central government, and hopefully it never will. The Parbati is one of the last major valleys of the state where the rhythms of nature have not yet been disturbed by the strident calls of "economic development" and, God willing, its virgin beauty will always remain untouched by the sordid hand of commerce. (In 2010, the state government declared the entire Parbati valley above Pulga, extending to the base of the Pin Parbat Pass, a national park—the Khirganga National Park. This area now enjoys the highest level of protection/conservation and, thankfully, no project will ever be permitted here. However, phase-II of the Parbati HEP, at the point where the Tosh Nullah meets the Parbati at Pulga, is under active consideration—the votaries of commerce will not be put off so easily!)

Continuing on the left bank of the Parbati, upstream of the confluence with Dibbi Bokri, one has to walk for another four kilometres to a desolate place called Pandupul. It gets its name from a huge, monolithic rock that straddles the river! It is an unbelievable sight for the river here must be all of 10 metres wide, a roaring torrent, its banks about five metres high, and perched on top of it is this one rock, its underbelly chiselled into an arch by the billions of cubic metres of water that have been flowing down since longer than man can remember. This rock serves as the bridge for crossing back to the right bank—rough steps have been cut into the rock face to facilitate the process. One has to clamber up on all fours about 10 feet to the top and then down again on the other side, hugging its smooth surface as if one's life depended on it, which it does for one slip and there's no way to go but down into the torrent. Local mythology has it that during their travels the Pandavas came to this point, and Bhim threw this rock across the river so that they could all cross it—hence the name Pandupul. The Pandavas liked the place and are reported to have even settled down here for a few years. It is perhaps not difficult to laugh at this quaint myth, but it is not easy either: all around Pandupul are terraced fields, levelled as if by some earth-moving machinery, in a terrain where one cannot otherwise find a 10 by 10 patch of flat land, or even one square foot that is not littered with rocks and boulders. There is no record of any community of peoples ever living or farming here, and indeed the climate would rule this out as Pandupul is at an elevation of about 13,000 feet and snowbound most of the year. So who made these terraced fields; who levelled the land? Nature? The Pandavas? Some unknown and unrecorded peoples in times bygone? We had no answers and we certainly didn't feel like laughing at the legend of the Pandavas.

It had been a long and tiring day—about 25 km of trekking. We decided to camp after crossing the river as the sun had started to set and it was beginning to get really cold. Pandupul is above the treeline and there are no trees or timber here to burn. The only thing that grows at this altitude is a bush called the *telu dhoop*, about two feet high but with a fair spread, whose roots are in great demand for making the aromatic *dhoop* and agarbattis (joss sticks). Given the heights at which it is found it is but natural that it grows very slowly, and can take 50 years to reach a height of two feet. The plant is well on its way to extinction in the state, thanks to the lethargy of the forest department and the avaricious cupidity of traders. Hundreds of quintals of this endangered herb are gathered from the high mountain ranges of the state each year and sold in the towns of Punjab at ridiculously low prices. This practice is ecologically unsustainable because the plants are taken out by their roots, since it is the root where its aromatic properties lie, and thus rendering natural regeneration impossible. Trekkers and pilgrims also play havoc with this unfortunate shrub for it is used as fuel and as a substitute for firewood above the treeline. The government needs to wake up and act quickly to save this precious aromatic herb—devise policies to educate the public, ban the export of this plant, and perhaps even provide fuel wood depots at the more frequented camping sites and passes so that an alternative is available and the need to burn *telu dhoop* is not felt.

The third day's trek takes one to the glacial lake of Mantalai, source of the river Parbati: the distance is about 16 km and can be covered in six hours quite comfortably. The trail goes up a one kilometre wide, gently inclining valley (at 4,116 metres, Mantalai is only about 400 metres higher than Pandupul) with the now adolescent Parbati playfully gurgling down its left side (right side as you go up the valley). The rest of the valley is surrendered to wide, incredibly green alpine pastures and meadows, almost knee-deep in multi-hued flowers, shrubs, and the ever-present *telu dhoop*: hiking through them is like taking a stroll through Eden. The valley is flanked on either side by towering snow-covered peaks, from which tumble small streams impatient to join the Parbati on its way down to the Beas—the pastures are criss-crossed with these small water courses. A month earlier we would have had to ford them, but in September we could easily hop across with the help of some strategically placed boulders. Knowing that this was an easy stage we took our time, stopping often to bask in the bright sunshine, absorbing a magnificence that all of us knew we would never see again,

fully conscious of the fact that very few human beings have ever set eyes on this almost untouched landscape. We had the whole valley to ourselves as all the Gaddis (shepherds) had moved down for the winters: we could see only one flock of sheep, distant specks on a mountainside across the river, and they too were moving down.

After about 14 km the valley gradually starts widening out even more and the Parbati spreads out into a delta, distributing itself into a score of water courses. This is an amazing sight because rivers originating at such great heights usually descend in furious torrents, and rarely have the space and gentle gradient to fan out into a delta. The delta is about a kilometre long and easy to negotiate. Above it the valley abruptly narrows and veers to the left, ending at a huge rockfall about a hundred metres high, appropriately called the Shahi Dwar or Royal Gateway: the river has carved its way through this on the right, but we had to climb the rocks. Cresting this mound we suddenly came face to face with the Mantalai Lake, the watery womb that is the birthplace of the Parbati. The first sight of Mantalai takes one's breath away, partly because of its sheer and unexpected size, and its awesome topography. The lake is nestled in a huge elliptical basin two kilometres long, stretching in a south-east–north-west alignment, and about half a kilometre at its widest point. It is enclosed by massive mountain features on all sides that were covered with snow even in September, giving the lake a grim and forbidding appearance, and imparting to its waters a pale, slate-coloured pallor, and a menacing stillness. There is only one small opening at the north-west end (the direction from which we had come) through which the river happily escapes from its forbidding cradle in a gushing torrent. At the opposite, south-east end the basin again narrows into a glaciated, boulder-and-moraine strewn valley, into which glaciers and small streams debouch in large numbers, feeding the lake. The lake is also fed by the innumerable streams flowing down from the glaciers and snowfields on the flanks of the surrounding mountain slopes. In winters the glaciers can come right down to the lake's perimeter, retreating again in the summers; the size of the lake thus differs with the seasons. Mantalai is a pure glacial lake and camping

PAGES 162–163:
The shrine at Mantalai Lake
Courtesy:
Sanjeeva Pandey

on its banks is a near spiritual experience, so overawed is one by the various facets and forces of Nature that are visible here. One cannot forget that this is the world of the mountains, the ice, and the wind, and the few human beings who occasionally wander in here are mere intruders who come to pay obeisance to the primeval forces of creation that live and rule here. Mantalai is not a pretty lake like Khajjiar, or scenic like Chandratal, or gentle like Renuka: it is a lake which is majestic in its grandeur, confident in its silence, and arrogant in its ruggedness. It commands respect not admiration. We camped on the shores of the lake in temperatures that dropped below freezing point at night. There is absolutely no vegetation here, not even the *telu dhoop*, so we had to make do with the ubiquitous Maggi noodles on our single kerosene stove. We were all uncomfortably aware that the really hard climbing would start the next day.

On the fourth day one has to cover only about nine kilometres, but it is still advisable to make an early start for reasons that shall be explained later. We got up at 6:00 am, had a perfunctory wash in the freezing waters of the lake, swallowed some *dalia* or porridge, and set off an hour later. We continued up the south-eastern end of the lake for about three kilometres, along the valley which feeds it. The valley, however, had now become anything but picturesque. This is a pure glaciated zone—the valley walls, which were actually the sides of the looming mountains, now stood barely 200 metres apart, maimed by the action of glaciers over hundreds of years, their innards laid bare; the valley floor is littered with boulders and moraine, through which the melting waters somehow find their way to the lake. Picking one's way through this moonscape is a tiring and not very pleasant exercise—it takes almost two hours to negotiate this stretch. After three or four kilometres the track leaves the valley to the left and turns eastwards, ending abruptly at an awe-inspiring feature. Straight ahead is a scree-covered slope rising at an impossible angle of 60-70 degrees, towering 1,000 feet into the sky: this is the first pass that has to be crossed on the way to Pin Parbat proper. There is no discernible track on this slope since it consists entirely of scree, loose boulders, and moraine;

it is difficult to find a secure foothold on this treacherous surface, and since the body is already fighting to maintain balance on this acutely tilted slope, negotiating this feature is a difficult and risky business. The only way to do it is by making wide traverses—about 50 to 60 feet each—across the face of the mountainside, zigzagging one's way upwards. One is constantly losing one's footing and sliding down. It

Another view of the Mantalai
Courtesy: Sanjeeva Pandey

takes about two hours to cover this vertical distance of 1,000 feet. Due to the weathering action of the sun and the wind, as the day progresses and both the temperature and the air currents pick up, it is common for small boulders to be dislodged from the top of the mountain. These start small avalanches, which in turn dislodge huge boulders that can come hurtling down at any time with minimal notice, proving to be

lethal. It is therefore advisable to keep one wary eye turned upwards to spot the slightest movement: sometimes rocks can be disturbed even by small animals. More importantly, it is prudent to cross this stretch and reach the top before noon, i.e. before the wind strength increases or the sun makes the rocks expand and move. I found this particular physical feature similar in every respect to the Charang Ghati Pass on the Kinner Kailash route, except for the fact that the latter has fewer rocks flying around and is therefore not as dangerous.

One need not climb all the way to the top of the feature—about 100 feet below the top the track branches off to the right and crosses the ridgeline over a rocky saddle. It takes four hours from Mantalai to reach the saddle; on attaining it we were presented with the most magnificent and panoramic view imaginable—a 270-degree vista stretching from the east to the north, consisting of an endless array of mighty snow-capped peaks to the west and north which feed the lonely river that we were about to leave. To the east are visible the mountains of the Pin Parbat range and the even mightier glaciers that lay hidden in their folds. So all-encompassing is the view that only a wide-angle camera can do justice to its grand beauty: we, of course, did not have one and had to content ourselves with taking a sequence of shots that we hoped we could piece together back home!

After a half-hour rest on the saddle we descended for an hour over a gentle slope, heading roughly eastwards, into a small valley through which meanders another one of the streams that flow into the Mantalai Lake. This is a special stream, however, because it originates directly from a huge glacier that sits astride the Pin Parbat Pass, which is quite visible from here. A kilometre into the valley and one reaches the site for Base Camp-I, the last halt before the pass—we reached this point at about 3:00 pm. We could have continued on for another three hours or so and covered more ground so as to reduce the distance to be travelled the next (and most difficult) day. However, it is advisable to camp here for the night as there are no proper camping sites available beyond this point, and it is too cold to camp at the base of the pass without specialised equipment, tenting gear, and maybe oxygen: since the pass is about another 2,000 feet higher than Base Camp-I, the less time one spends at such extreme heights the better. It is risky to spend an entire night either at the pass or immediately below; moreover, the weather at these heights can, and does, change for the worse without any warning—getting caught in a blizzard, or even a storm or snowfall here can be fatal. One should, before attempting a high pass, always pitch the last camp at a site beyond the influence of the weather on the pass itself. This way, one always has the option of aborting the crossing if the weather takes a turn for the worse. (In fact, when we reached Base Camp-I we could see that it was snowing on the pass, and we fervently hoped that the storm would clear by night so that we could make our crossing the next day). Some parties do leave Mantalai and cross the pass on the same day, camping on the other side, which means another six hours of climbing and trekking from Base Camp-I! One has to be extremely fit and in top physical condition to attempt this, and even then there is an element of risk and foolhardiness in doing so—one would be crossing the pass at about 4:00 or 5:00 pm, which is extremely dangerous and goes against all mountain lore and wisdom. All high mountain passes should be crossed before noon as the weather invariably deteriorates after that, and getting caught in a snowstorm on such a high pass means almost certain death: people have died crossing the Pin Parbat. Furthermore, there is no safe camping site on the other side of the Pin Parbat for almost two hours, and there is every chance of one being overtaken by darkness before reaching the campsite. Therefore, while some parties have done it in one day from Mantalai, I would strongly advise against it. Trekking should be fun and enjoyable, not needlessly risky and dangerous. So we pitched our tents at Base Camp-I, snoozed in the bright sunlight, had another makeshift dinner when darkness descended, and retired early.

It was bitterly cold at night and any sleep difficult to come by. However, we awoke on the fifth day to a blindingly brilliant and crisp dawn: the storm on the pass had blown over at night and we could see, even from this distance, that it had left a fresh layer of snow on the saddle and the surrounding peaks. This was not necessarily good news

The snout of a gigantic glacier below the pass. It looks like the Bhakra Dam!

since a fresh layer of snow would cover the crevasses and make them that much more difficult to spot. This was going to be a tough day of trekking—not only did we have to ascend to the pass (5,319 metres), but en route we had to traverse two glaciers and then descend another 1,000 metres to Base Camp-II on the other side. It is advisable to make an early start, latest by 7:00 am. Initially one follows the stream up the valley for about half a kilometre; the valley then is squeezed shut by a huge rockfall about a kilometre in length and 200 metres in height. On the right (or southern) side of this rockfall is the snout of a massive glacier about 50 metres high, the source of the stream we had been following. So massive is its size that we felt like we were moving along the toe of the Bhakra Dam! The snout was full of caves and overhangs from which emerged innumerable trickles of melting water, joining together to form the little stream. It is an awe-inspiring sight of nature at work and one cannot but be humbled by its sheer mechanics: how this forbidding and raw power of nature is converted into a substance that sustains all life on this planet, including our own puny beings who squander this same substance without a thought given to the interplay of immense primeval forces that have resulted in its creation.

Climbing along the rockfall one soon ascends above the glacier, which now reveals itself in all its magnificent glory—it was about a kilometre wide in an East–West alignment and stretched as far as the eye could see towards the south. We were glad that our route took us along its snout and that we did not have to traverse it as the glacier was fissured with huge crevasses, hundreds in number, and crossing them would have been an extremely dangerous proposition. On reaching the crest of the rockfall we encountered a scree-covered slope from where, for the first time, we had a clear view of the saddle of the Pin Parbat Pass, completely encased by another huge glacier, rising like an ice wall on the ridgeline. We all knew that this was one glacier we couldn't avoid and had to cross, and the knowledge was none too reassuring! We reached the toe of this glacier after another hour of tough climbing: the ice wall was about 10 feet high at this point and our guide had to cast around for about half an hour before he could locate the exact point at which we had to begin the crossing. The Pin Parbat Pass is one of the most difficult passes in Himachal precisely because locating the route over it is not easy. Most high mountain passes are shaped like a saddle—a low ridge between two higher points or outcrops—and therefore easy to identify. But the Pin Parbat top is just one huge, undulating glacier, a vast field of ice that never melts, and one has to judge one's way across it. There is no obvious or discernible track and only an experienced guide can spot the way. A wrong assessment and the unfortunate trekker can wander for days on the monstrous glacier, injury and death being almost certain from freezing or falling into any one of the innumerable crevasses. The Pin Parbat is not to be taken lightly.

We immediately realised that snowfall from the previous night had made our task more difficult and risky: the fresh, powdery snow had settled lightly over the huge snowfield, concealing the crevasses

Trekking party crossing the saddle of Pin Parbat Pass (author is fourth from right). This picture was taken moments before the author fell into a crevasse!

and fissures that would otherwise have been visible. This mantle of white gave a false impression of solidity and our guide knew that this impression was treacherous; he therefore insisted that all members of the party (12 in number) should rope themselves together—a decision that probably saved two lives, including mine. Though we moved in strict single file with the most experienced members in front carving out a trail through the two-foot-thick snow, careful to put our feet in the footprints of the person ahead, two of us (including I) fell into crevasses. Fortunately, the crevasses were just about two feet wide, and when we fell into them our heavy backpacks wedged into the lips of the fissures, preventing us from sliding in completely. This gave the other members of the party enough time to haul on the ropes and pull us out. After this incident, however, I have come to realise how useful a backpack can be even as a safety equipment: had it not been for the rucksack I would have plummeted into the silent depths of the crevasse, probably snapping the rope or taking another couple of the party down with me. Apart from this particular incident I have found that if one slips while trekking or climbing a slope, a rucksack can be useful in breaking the fall or in absorbing the impact of the fall. I now make it a point to carry my own rucksack, even if there are porters who can do it.

We were extra careful after these couple of close encounters and continued our gentle ascent of the glacier for another hour without any further mishap. Quite suddenly, we were at the top of the glacier and on the Pin Parbat Pass (5,319 metres)! This is glacier-land indeed—we counted as many as 12 of them all around us. We were now standing on the watershed line between Kullu and Lahaul-Spiti districts; on the other side of the pass is the even more mysterious and intriguing Pin valley, taking its name from the Pin River. Originating from one of the glaciers we could see, it was the river we would be joining before the end of the day and one that would keep us company for the next three days. It was about 2:00 pm when we reached the pass and though the weather was fine, we decided not to tarry. We began our descent into Pin valley over another, smaller glacier that very soon gave way to the moraine and scree that we had got used to by now. From here on the descent is quite

PAGES 172–173: *Glaciers of the Pin Parbat range* Courtesy: Sanjeeva Pandey

The amazing hues of Pin valley. The Pin River is the white line running across the middle

steep, and we could see the Pin River far below, a silver stripe about a thousand metres below the pass. It took us about four hours and by 6:00 pm we had reached the site for Base Camp-II, a small meadow on the banks of the Pin which at this point is just a pretty brook about 10 metres wide and knee-deep. We were now at 4,200 metres, still far above the treeline, but grasses and some ferns were now visible. The entire party was absolutely exhausted, as much by the descent as by the climb to the pass, but we were also exhilarated at having scaled the pass, and so we spent the last of the kerosene in cooking up a regular dinner of rice and dal. Of course, it helped to know that we would be able to get firewood the next day.

We slept well that night on the banks of the bubbling Pin, confident in the knowledge that the most difficult part of the trek was behind us. We got up leisurely to a breathtaking view. Behind us, to the west, was the huge massif of the Pin Parbat that we had crossed the previous day. Straight ahead to the east the Pin valley rolled itself out in range after range of undulating mountains, all bathed in the golden glow of a rising sun, transforming the ice fields on Pin Parbat to a mantle of molten gold. It is 22 km from here to Samdoh, the next camping point. One begins the journey by fording the Pin about half a kilometre below the camp to cross over to its left bank (as there is no path on the right bank). From here on we would stick to the left bank all the way to Mudh, the last (or first) village in the Pin valley. In September the waters of the Pin were only knee high, but fast flowing and freezing cold: there is no danger involved in the crossing but one should avoid staying in the water for too long! Like all high mountain streams, it is advisable to ford it well before mid-morning as snowmelt increases later in the day and the level of the river rises. For the next eight kilometres the track clings to the grassy mountainside, barely eight inches wide, with the Pin now flowing a hundred feet below, gaining in both volume and sound. The valley here is about half a kilometre wide, its walls covered with grasses and shrubs of various colours that give the mountains of Spiti their distinct and unique range of hues: changing from black to yellow to grey to angry shades of orange and red. Providing the perfect backdrop to this riot of colours are the towering, snow-capped peaks on all sides, the jealous sentinels of this stark, savagely beautiful land.

After about eight kilometres the character of the track changes: the valley now broadens out considerably, and wide, scree-covered slopes interject themselves between the river and the valley walls. This is obviously a glaciated zone for the valley walls and slopes are all well-rounded, and the scree and moraine are detritus left behind by the retreating glaciers. The track passes over this rocky landscape for the next 12 km or so, and though it leads steadily downhill, it is arduous work going over these stones and boulders as the sun can be pretty hot in this rarefied atmosphere. Surprisingly, there is a lot of climbing still to be done. There are at least a dozen streams flowing down from the left to join the Pin. In the process they have carved out

Pin River with Mudh village in the middle ground

deep ravines through the moraine, each about 40 or 50 feet deep, and one has to continuously move in and out of them. The streams are too torrential to be forded and one has to negotiate them by hopping from one semi-submerged boulder to another—fortunately there is no shortage of boulders in this terrain! Nonetheless, some balance and skill is required if one does not wish to get soaked or sustain a sprain. There is a half-kilometre stretch that is extremely dangerous and must be negotiated with utmost care. Landslides have almost obliterated the track here: loose, slippery soil has been exposed on the steep slope and the footing is very insecure. It's almost a straight drop to the Pin about 250 feet below. The golden rule of trekking applies here: don't look down.

About seven to eight hours after leaving Base Camp-II one reaches the sixth day's camping point at Samdoh (3,700 metres), nothing but a slightly more open, grass-covered patch in an otherwise windblown location. But there are plenty of huge rocks in the shelter of which one can pitch tents. It is a regular Gaddi camping point, and they had even left behind some of their goods and gear when departing for their winter sojourn to warmer climes. This included a can of kerosene and a *tawa* for making chapatis or unleavened bread. We were careful not to touch the kerosene, though we did make good use of the *tawa*! Directly across from the campsite, on the opposite bank of the Pin, is the mouth of a huge valley that slants away in a south-easterly direction towards high, snow-covered peaks just about visible from the camp. This is the famous Bhaba valley, a popular, four-day trek: proceeding up the valley, one has to cross the Bhaba Pass, and finally end up at a place called Kafnu in the Kinnaur district. We could make out a well-marked track snaking its way into the valley, the precursor of the road coming from Mudh (more on that later).

The seventh day provides, by far, the best day's trekking on the entire route. Though one has to cover a distance of about 20 km to Mudh village, the walk is easy and at a gentle downward incline. The first couple of kilometres are through the same rock-and-moraine terrain one has become accustomed to, but after that the transformation is dramatic, giving way to vast undulating pastures sloping down to the river. These are carpeted with vegetation of a myriad hues, lending to the landscape the touch of a careless, masterful artist. This lush expanse is broken only by the streams flowing down to the Pin, though not as many as on the previous day. It really is a most pleasant walk all the way down to Mudh, which comes into view from a distance of five kilometres. However, the beauty of this stretch can be deceptive. Our guide informed us that just a couple of years ago, on this same stretch, a party of three foreigners and a dozen porters was caught in a sudden snowstorm (it was in late October, rather late for attempting this trek). The foreigners, who were better equipped in terms of boots and clothing, and carrying lighter loads, somehow managed to reach Mudh in the storm. The unfortunate porters decided to wait out the storm, without any form of protection in those flat grasslands. The storm developed into a blizzard that lasted for two days, preventing any rescue attempts by the villagers. By the time the storm cleared and the villagers could venture out, all the porters had frozen to death. There is beauty here but one must also remember that the inexorable forces of nature rule this primeval landscape, and nature has no patience for any form of weakness. The entire stretch from Pin Parbat to Mudh village is also part of the Pin Valley National Park, created to preserve the rare forms of wildlife indigenous to this region—the magnificent snow leopard, the Spiti wolf, the splendidly trophied ibex, and the ghoral (another species of mountain goat). However, it is only the very fortunate trekker who can spot these animals for they are extremely shy and stay away from the trekking corridors. But there have been sightings, especially of the ibex and ghoral—the best chance of doing so is very early in the mornings when the first rays of the sun hit the crags and peaks, as these animals come out then to bask in the warmth of the sun. The sighting of a snow leopard, of course, is extremely rare.

Some years ago a villager found two abandoned snow leopard cubs, their mother probably killed by poachers. He handed them over to officials of the forest department, a gift worth its weight in gold for wildlife conservationists. The male cub died after a few days; the female survived and was shifted to the Kufri Nature Park just outside Shimla. She was named Rosie by her keeper, and soon became the biggest attraction in the nature park with more than a hundred thousand visitors queuing up to see her each year. But typical bureaucratic apathy and political short-sightedness had already dictated her fate. A priceless opportunity to mate her in captivity (there were male snow leopards in the Darjeeling Zoo) was not availed of because of wranglings between the two state forest departments and the zoo authority of India. The unhygienic environs of the Kufri Nature Park, with its 800 ponies depositing tonnes of dung on the open road just outside the park, soon led to this splendid animal, its genes used to the clean, germ-free environment of the Spiti and Pin valleys, contracting an infection. The park authorities, possessing no hospital or even a medical officer, were unaware of this till Rosie was found dead in her cage one day. This was in the year 2002. An expert group went into the causes of her death and found that the unclean conditions in the area were responsible for the infection that eventually led to her demise. Even eight years later, however, the state government has taken no steps to improve conditions in Kufri. The number of ponies has, in fact, doubled since then!

Mudh is a village of only 40 houses but many more yaks, *churu* (cross between a yak and a cow), and horses. An ancient monastery perched precariously on a crumbling sand dune greets one when entering the village. Mudh produces premium potatoes and seeds in the vast, sloping acreages that surround the village, and has very promising agricultural potential. Its constraint in realising this potential, however, is the fact that it is 12 km from the nearest roadhead at Mikim, and the cost of transporting produce there on headload or horses would make the whole business unviable. At the moment, therefore, the honest citizens of Mudh practise a subsistence form of agriculture, and breed the famous Pin or Spiti ponies, also known as Chamurthi, for added income. These are a small, compact, and extremely hardy breed of ponies, well-suited and totally adapted to the mountain conditions. The horses that take tourists for a ride on the Ridge in Shimla or in

Kufri belong to this breed. I was told that the British also reared them as polo ponies, although whether this is still the practice I could not find out. Practically every family in Mudh breeds these ponies: once a year the surplus horses are taken to either the Lavi Mela at Rampur or to Chango in Kinnaur district and sold for as much as 25,000 to 30,000 rupees each. The sale of one or two ponies each year suffices to meet the cash requirements of a family. The citizens of Mudh may not be prosperous, and life can occasionally be harsh, but they lead a decent, self-sufficient, and fairly comfortable existence in this remote valley, in complete harmony with nature and their unique environment. We were lucky to spend one night at the house of a local resident, and for dinner partook of a wild mushroom curry called Shyamo. Now, the only exotic mushroom one had tasted was the Gucchi, which is priced at about 15,000–20,000 rupees per kilo in Delhi, but can be bought in the valleys of Kullu for about 2,000 rupees. Shyamo, however, was many notches above the Gucchi in sheer taste and flavour, and had a smooth, meat-like texture. Of course, it had to be washed down with the local liquor distilled from barley. Few evenings have provided me with more pleasure or lasting memories than the evening spent in Mudh. The future of this idyllic place is bright because the government has begun construction of a road that will connect Mikim, the present roadhead on the road from Kaza, with Kafnu in the Bhaba valley, across the Bhaba Pass in Kinnaur. This road will pass through Mudh and much of the area we trekked through on days six and seven, enter the Bhaba valley, which we had seen from our camp at Samdoh, and follow the trekking track to Kafnu. This would open up the magnificent Pin valley to tourists, and Mudh shall finally emerge from its splendid isolation of centuries. The prospect, I must admit, generates some misgivings in me for the Himachal government's track record in protecting its priceless ecology from rampant, destructive tourism has not been encouraging. And this is an environment so fragile that it does not take much thoughtless intervention to cause irreparable damage.

This road, however, has got held up because of objections by the burghers of Kafnu, and for a peculiar reason! The Spiti side of Bhaba Pass is barren and devoid of any vegetation while the Kinnaur or Kafnu side has good forests of conifers and oaks. For generations now, the residents of Mudh and Chudh have been meeting their timber and wood requirements by smuggling it from Kinnaur surreptitiously on the hardy yaks, over the pass and the narrow trails—a difficult but rewarding enterprise. The residents of Kafnu are apprehensive, quite rightly in my opinion, that the construction of a road across the Bhaba Pass will exponentially increase this activity and denude their own forests. This dispute in Eden has held up this road, and the conservationists are secretly delighted for a motorable road through this fragile national park can only spell disaster. One also wonders whether approval of the Supreme Court appointed Central Empowered Committee (CEC) has been obtained for this road through a protected area.

The eighth day is the final day of the trek; by now even the most intrepid trekker would be looking forward to its conclusion—to a hot bath and shave, a change of fresh clothes, and a bed that does not have to be zipped up! It's a four hours' comfortable walk to the terminal point of the trek, the twin villages of Sagnam-Mikim (3,600 metres) at the confluence of the Pin and the Paraiho. Descending about 50 metres from Mudh to the left bank of the Pin, which skirts the village about 200 metres away, one goes along the riverbank for about five kilometres, passing below the village of Tailing high up on a promontory on the opposite bank. At this point the track was blocked by huge landslides caused by the construction of the Sagnam–Mudh road, forcing us to cross over to the right bank on a wire-and-pulley bridge. There is no romance and magic left in the journey any more: this is a well-trodden path, and all the signs indicated that we were nearing the urbanised antithesis of the nature and isolation that we had been part of for the last eight days. The earlier magnificence, splendour, and vibrant hues of the Pin valley, the mysterious, silent, looming peaks—these were all in the past now and gave way to a couple of tractors, hordes of mules and ponies carrying provisions, scattered buildings and electricity poles. We wished for the trek to end quickly so that we could continue to retain in our mind's eye and in our memory the Pin valley of the first seven days. At a place called Khar we crossed back to the left bank of the Pin, arriving at Sagnam-Mikim. This is a fairly large twin village with a large number of houses, shops, government offices, schools, and a comfortable PWD rest house. At this point the Paraiho, a sizeable stream, joins the Pin. The Paraiho originates from the Dibbi Bokri feature described earlier: one can also travel up this stream to join the Parbati below Pandupul. But this is a lesser-known trek, its dangers and difficulties not well-known or documented, and therefore it is best left alone. At Mikim there is one last bridge to be crossed over the Paraiho, and one is on the motorable, single-lane road that leads to the sub-divisional headquarters of Kaza, 35 km away. From Kaza one carries on to Manali over the Kunzum and Rohtang passes.

2000

TO LE

BARALACHA PASS

CAM

SURAJ TAL

DARCHA

TOPKOYO

CAM

R. BHAGA

BARA LACHA GLACIER

TO PANGI

KEYLONG

TANDI

T

SAMUDRA TAPU

R. CHANDRABHAGA

CHOTA DHARA

CHATRU

ROHTANG PASS

KOKSAR

R. CHANDRA

GULABA

HANTA STREAM

TO HA

MANALI

MAP NOT TO SCALE

═ MOTORABLE ROAD

— TREKKING ROUTE

// PASS

• VILLAGE/CAMPING SITE

~ RIVER/STREAM

◯ LAKE

///// GLACIER

N

Chandratal to Baralacha-Pass

handratal (lake of the moon) is one of the most beautiful water bodies in Himachal, and though it is situated at a discouraging height of 4,270 metres, it also happens to be one of the most accessible. Located in the Lahaul part of the Lahaul-Spiti district, it actually lies between the massive Rohtang (13,500 feet) and Kunzum (16,000 feet) passes, perched on the floodplains of the Chandra River whose valley divides the two. It is about six hours by road from Manali via the Rohtang Pass. Rohtang is not very high as Himalayan passes go, but it is one of the most forbidding and dangerous ones. There are two reasons for this. First, its weather: separating, as it does, the lush, densely forested valleys of Kullu from the cold and stark deserts of Lahaul-Spiti, Rohtang creates its own unpredictable and treacherous weather patterns. Strong winds blow incessantly on the pass and the weather can deteriorate in minutes from bright sunshine to blizzard, particularly in the winter months when as much as 20 feet of snow can pile up. The second feature that makes Rohtang so dangerous is its physical profile. Unlike other passes such as Charang Ghati or Kugti or even Thamsar, which consist of a narrow saddle between two higher features and would typically take five minutes to cross, the saddle

on Rohtang is almost a kilometre long and half as wide! This means that it takes much longer to cross the hump, making one vulnerable to any sudden change in the weather. This can prove to be fatal in the winters as even a few minutes of snowfall can completely obscure the road or track. Most people who perish on this pass (and a few do every year) are later found to have been going around in doomed circles till they finally succumbed to exhaustion and hypothermia.

There is something sinister in the very sound of these two syllables: ROH-TANG. And well might ancient armies have thought so for Rohtang means "the field of corpses". It probably got this dreaded title from the fact that thousands of soldiers of the armies of Maharaja Ranjit Singh, Raja Sansar Chand, and the Gurkhas perished here in their efforts to conquer the valley of Lahaul. In fact, the tiny hamlet of Gulaba, 15 km from Manali on the way to Rohtang, is named after one of Ranjit Singh's most famous generals, Gulaba Singh, who is reported to have died on the battlefield here. Today, Gulaba is better known as the site of one of the most infamous and devastating experiments in the history of Himachal's forestry management.

Till about 40 years ago this area contained a dense forest of birch, fir, and spruce spread over hundreds of acres. Then, in the 1960s and 1970s, mechanised logging was introduced here and "clearfelling" carried out—thousands of the priceless trees, which had taken hundreds of years to reach maturity in this rarefied environment, were slaughtered. No mother tree or seed bearers were left, rendering natural regeneration impossible. Realising its mistake too late, the forest department established nurseries for these species at Kullu and Shamshi with the intention of replanting the Gulaba area. But saplings raised in the warmer climes of Kullu and Shamshi could not adapt when transplanted in Kothi and Gulaba. The programme was a massive failure and the whole stretch is today an Elliotsian wasteland, the thousands of pathetic stumps mute testimony to a state's greed and a department's folly. IFS probationers are now brought here from Dehradun to see for themselves how forestry should NOT be practised! Of late some natural regeneration of deodar (cedar) and *kail* (blue pine) has started taking place, but the magnificent fir and spruce forests have gone for ever from this area. They will never return for the micro-climate itself has changed perceptibly as a result of the denudation, and their climatic niche has now disappeared permanently.

From Rohtang the road winds its way down 10 km to Koksar (10,500 feet). It can be termed the base camp for Rohtang on the northern side, just as Marhi discharges this function on the southern or Manali side. Koksar is basically a collection of shops, dhabas, workshops, and a couple of govt offices. It is a staging point for the thousands of trucks carrying all manner of supplies to Lahaul-Spiti and Ladakh, and presents the perfect picture of a frontier town—rough and tough, but with the rare camaraderie of regulars on a dangerous route; there is also a sense of lurking danger from the elements, which fosters transient friendships even between strangers. It has a capacious and well-appointed PWD rest house, a godsend for the travellers who may have to take refuge here when the Rohtang is closed suddenly due to snowfall. The local people of Lahaul-Spiti sometimes venture to cross the pass in the winters, even though it may be closed to vehicular traffic. They take a very deliberate risk in doing so: spending the night in Koksar, they usually begin the climb at 2:00 or 3:00 am since the weather is usually clear at this time, the ice is firm, and there are fewer chances of avalanches. They go straight up along tracks marked before the road was built, or follow the electricity pylons, and stop for nothing. The overriding concern is to cross the pass before the weather turns. If it does, and someone lags behind for whatever reason, no one will stop for him: fathers have been known to abandon their sons in such circumstances. A couple of people die in this attempt every year, their bodies usually found in the summers when the snow melts.

Koksar is located on the nearer or left bank of the Chandra River as it flows down in an East–West alignment. There is a Bailey bridge across the river here, which one crosses and turns left (west) to carry on to Keylong, the capital of Lahaul, about 45 km away, and further on to Ladakh and Leh, another 300 km or so. But to go to Chandratal (and to Spiti and Kaza) one has to proceed east, up the Chandra valley on the

left bank to Chhatru (15 km), Chhota Dhara (30 km), Bara Dhara, and Batal (40 km), then northwards for the last eight kilometres to the lake. None of these places has any habitation as such, though Chhatru does have a PWD rest house and Batal has a big dhaba run by an enterprising Nepali lady. The dhaba, however, is purely seasonal and has to close with the first snowfall, which can be any time after the first week of October; it opens only when the Rohtang and Kunzum passes are opened for traffic, usually by the end of May or beginning of June.

The road eastwards from Koksar follows the Chandra upstream all the way to Batal, first on the left bank but crossing over to the right bank at Chhatru. The road is in very bad shape and recommended only for SUVs or MUVs. This road connects Lahaul to the rest of Himachal, and is the only artery for taking in supplies and carrying out Lahaul's agricultural produce, including the famous seed potatoes and peas (and, increasingly, apples). Added to this fairly heavy traffic is the fact that the road lies under more than six to ten feet of snow for almost five months of the year, and one can understand why it is in such bad shape—it is almost impossible to maintain. The route is completely barren and desolate, rocky and with no sign of life. Chhatru, Chhota Dhara, and Bara Dhara are not places but only reference points for the traveller, and especially for rescue teams in the winters. It can, and does, become a death trap in the winters for the unfortunate traveller if he is caught in a sudden snowfall; trapped between the two high passes, he can neither go back nor forward. A few fatalities each year is almost the norm here. In one such interesting incident about 15 years ago, a government employee going to Manali on foot was stranded at Chhatru in a blizzard for 129 days! He took shelter in the old rest house there, which was deserted (the chowkidar had already left for the winters) but was stocked with provisions. There was, however, no fuel. The poor chap spent the next four months there all alone, and since there was no fuel for cooking or heating, he gradually took apart the wooden rest house, plank by plank. This enabled him to survive the winter, and when the passes opened in the spring the first travellers on the road were horrified to encounter a black, hairy creature rushing at them at

Chhatru, waving his arms and shouting incoherently! They pelted it with stones, mistaking it for a bear, till they realised who it was. This must be one of the most unusual stories of survival in these harsh climes and has almost become part of the folklore here. However, not every trapped traveller is so lucky.

About a kilometre after Chhatru a deep gorge meets the Chandra from the right, or south, from which a huge torrent of water debouches into the river. This is the Hamta stream, culminating its journey that begins at a glacier about eight kilometres from this confluence, just below the Hamta Pass; the waters of this stream are crystal clear and in sharp contrast to the muddy flow of the Chandra. Just before the confluence of the Chandra and the Hamta Nullah, another substantial body of water joins the river from the left, or north. This is the Chhatru Nullah fed by the Chhatru glacier, a massive montane glacier perched high above the valley. It is not clearly visible from the road but can be seen from the other side of the Chandra when coming down the Hamta Nullah from Hamta pass. Between Chhatru and Batal, looking southwards or to one's right, one can spot the Chhota Shigri and Bara Shigri glaciers, more than a kilometre away and above the left bank of the Chandra. The local people will inform you that just about 20 years or so ago, these massive glaciers stretched all the way down to the river itself! That these glaciers have receded is established even by satellite imagery, and these two have been picked by the Himachal Pradesh government for detailed studies so as to assess precisely the effects of global warming on the glaciers in the state. We could only see the Bara Shigri in October, which is certainly not a good sign.

At Batal we crossed the Chandra on a Bailey bridge and turned sharply northwards onto the non-metalled road leading to Chandratal. If one continues due eastwards on the main road one would reach the Kunzum Pass, just 12 km away—the gateway to Spiti. The dirt track to Chandratal is well-aligned and has a good surface; it hugs the mountain slopes on the left bank of the river, about 100 metres above it, and is quite narrow. There are few points on this stretch where two vehicles can cross, but fortunately the dust plume of an approaching vehicle can be seen from a distance and an adequately wide spot found in time. The valley of the Chandra here is huge, at least half a kilometre wide, comprising only of rocks, shale, and dirt; there is not a blade of grass to be seen anywhere. After about seven kilometres the road turns eastwards and leaves the Chandra. At about this point the protected Chandratal Wetland area begins, which is in the control and management of the forest department. Till about the year 2003, no vehicles were allowed beyond this point and visitors had to hike the last four kilometres to the lake. But we found that

The mirror-like surface of Chandratal lake reflecting the surrounding mountains

these restrictions had been removed in 2004—a very unfortunate and blinkered decision as the last lap to the lake is over gently ascending grasslands whose green cover (a rarity at these heights) should be preserved. By allowing vehicles to drive over these plains this green cover is being rapidly eroded and the entire stretch is at grave risk of

becoming a dust bowl. Every vehicle raises huge clouds of dust which further smother the environment.

About 40 minutes after leaving Batal, we topped a slight mound and suddenly saw this blue, elongated pendant of water spread out below us. The first sight of Chandratal (14,500 feet) is a visual shock, caused by the totally incongruent presence of an iridescent, dazzling blue feature embedded in a landscape that is uniformly brown, yellow, and dry. The lake lies in a roughly north-west to south-east alignment. It looks smaller than it actually is, mainly because its northern part is hidden by a slight promontory of land jutting in from its western flank. We walked round it and found that its circumference was about four kilometres! Nobody knows how deep the lake is; its waters, as can be expected, are extremely cold. Swimming in it is not recommended, no matter how good a swimmer one is. For one, its banks are extremely precipitous and drop away to the depths without any warning. Secondly, and even more important, the freezing waters can suddenly numb your senses and the nervous system, rendering the swimmer immobile. There are many reported cases of swimmers, usually foreigners, swimming out 50 metres or so into the lake, suddenly realising that their bodies are becoming numb, and desperately trying to swim back; they usually don't make it. The lake claims a victim every year or so. There are no visible signs of any aquatic life in the lake—some years ago the fisheries department had introduced trout and carp seedlings here, apparently without any success. But, intriguingly, we saw a heron near the lake; perhaps some life forms do exist here. Most people assume that Chandratal is the source of Chandra River, which is not at all true. The river flows down its valley about one kilometre to the west of the lake, and the two are separated by a ridge. Although there is no scientifically authenticated elucidation for the origin of the lake, it is generally believed that the original alignment of the Chandra River was more to the east, that the lake was part of this original course. At some point in time, natural phenomenon or change shifted the river to the west, leaving the lake portion stranded as a separate water body. In any case, it is now fed by snowmelt from the surrounding mountains, and

for all we know there might even be an underground spring or aquifer feeding it from below. There is only one small outlet for the water, a small channel towards its south-eastern end that ultimately drains into the river itself.

Chandratal has been officially classified as one of four protected wetlands in the state; the other three are Pong Dam, Khajjiar Lake, and Renuka Lake. The altitude of Chandratal, however, is by far the greatest, and this alone makes its environment the most fragile and endangered. It is supposed to be administered by the forest department, and funds for its protection and development are made available by the central government and the department of science and technology of the state. However, a single visit to the lake is enough to convince anyone that the concerned authorities have no clue as to how to manage this priceless natural asset. The lake is visited by hundreds of tourists each year, but no attempt has been made to assess the carrying capacity of its environs and to regulate the numbers accordingly: when we reached Chandratal we were shocked to see that at least 100 students were camped there in about 15 tents right at the edge of the lake, which should never be allowed as the pollutants flow straight into the water body. No tenting sites have been developed; there is only one pit latrine, and absolutely no one around to ensure that the visitors behave in a responsible manner. There is no arrangement for collecting or disposing of the garbage that is inevitably generated. Some years back the forest department had mooted a proposal to establish an ecotourism society (consisting mainly of local tribals) to manage this place, but it appears to have made no progress.

We camped the first night on the shores of the lake, an absolutely unforgettable experience: the bright moonlight and starlight reflecting off the white surrounding peaks, and the placid waters of the lake created a tapestry of midnight blue, sequin dotted with silver as it were! It was extremely cold, as can be imagined since this was the middle of October. Fortunately, private entrepreneurship was not lacking even at this remote location. One young man from Baijnath called Babloo had set up a dhaba here under a huge parachute (!)

whose material, we found, was much more effective in stopping the
wind than the usual tarpaulins. It could accommodate 15 persons with
ease, and since it also served as the kitchen, was quite warm. We spent
a wonderful evening in this parachute dhaba with Babloo serving up a
very decent meal of eggs, dal, rice, chapattis, and potatoes. He made
a decent living, he informed, between May and October, catering to
the tourists and campers who came to Chandratal. His charges were
also reasonable considering that everything had to be brought here
from either Manali or Keylong, the last few kilometres on horses
or headload: he charged 30 rupees for a night in the tent (sleeping
bag provided), and a meal cost about the same. Very few people,
however, actually spent a night at this place, and these too were usually
foreigners. On a good day Babloo would cater to between 30 and 40

The author standing before Chandratal lake at the first light of dawn visitors. By the end of October he would pack up and go back to the milder climes and lush valleys of his native Baijnath in Kangra district, to his parents and family. He is one of a remarkable breed of native entrepreneurs; on practically all my treks I have encountered people like Babloo who would sense a niche of opportunity, and would go hundreds of miles to set up shop in the most desolate and remote locations to ply a profitable but lonely trade. I have seen them in Merh in Bara Bhangal, in Kheer Ganga en route to Pin Parbat, at Bhim Dwar below Srikhand Mahadev, and many other places too. They also provide an essential service to the weary trekker who is short on supplies or not fully equipped for these inhospitable terrains.

Floodplains of the Chandra River above Chandratal

The track from Chandratal climbs gently in a west-north-west direction over pastures degraded by the thousands of sheep that flock here in the summers. To the west are a range of mighty peaks rising

to 20,000-22,000 feet, most of which still remain unscaled. They are part of the Chandrabhaga (CB) range and are numbered as CB1, CB2, and so on. One could see the summits of CB13 and CB14 where, in 2003, the remains of a military plane that had crashed in the 1980s were found by some trekkers. All its occupants—about a hundred soldiers and crew—had been killed in the crash, everything swallowed up and covered by the impenetrable snow. For more than 20 years the disappearance of the plane remained a mystery, till the moving glaciers and melting snows disgorged their hoary repast in 2003. These eternal mountains do not give up their secrets easily and time has no meaning for them. They have taken millions of years to rise; what, after all, is a few score years? It is only we humans, with short lives and shorter visions that worry about time. Beyond the CB range lie the Keorang (KR) and the Mulkila ranges, a succession of marching peaks that accompany one all the way to Baralacha. Four kilometres from Chandratal one again encounters the Chandra River, which we had left a couple of kilometres below the lake on the previous day. The river valley here is a huge floodplain, almost a kilometre wide, and the river flows in a number of channels. One walks not on the valley floor itself but on a faint track on the valley wall on its left bank. After another three kilometres or so, a huge, towering ridge begins to appear in the middle of the valley, forcing the river to divide into two streams. This ridge, which is about 10 km long, is actually an island in the river and is known as Samudra Tapu. Completely covered with ice in the winters, it must present an awe-inspiring sight then; when we saw it, however, it was just a barren, rocky, lifeless promontory. (About two weeks after we passed through this area a group of scientists claimed to have seen a UFO over the *tapu*).

The track is rocky and dusty but not difficult. A large number of gullies and arroyos carry snowmelt from the mountains on one's right to the river, and one has to constantly go in and out of them. We saw no animals except for pica and a marmot, but we did see a number of birds—horned lark, a solitary lammergeyer vulture with its massive nine-foot wingspan, wagtails, black redstart, sand lark, snow pigeons, and the crow-like choughs (which were the most abundant and fearless of all). After about 20 km and eight hours we reached Topkogongma, our campsite for the second night. *Topko* means river and *gongma* means lower, so Topkogongma means "the lower river". The reference is not to river Chandra but to a small stream that comes from the right at this spot to join the Chandra. The campsite is just above and before this stream, which has to be crossed the next day en route to Baralacha Pass. It could not be forded at the time we reached there, at about five in the evening, since the snowmelt had turned it into a raging torrent; fording it then would have been a risky proposition. So we camped above its banks at an altitude of about 15,000 feet or 4,500 metres. It gets dark here pretty quickly for the towering peaks on either side intercept the rays of the sun well before it sets, and it is also very windy and cold—not a very attractive or hospitable place. We were extremely tired after

Crossing the
Topkogongma

eight hours of continuous trekking and thus, after a makeshift dinner, everyone retired to their tents, quite a change from the social bonhomie of the previous evening in Babloo's tent at Chandratal!

The sun rises early at these altitudes and it is advisable to ford the Topkogongma before 7:00 am. We awoke early on the third day, and crossed it quite easily as the waters had receded considerably and now only came up to our thighs. But they were so cold it knocked the breath from our bodies! The trek on the other side of Topkogongma resumes on the left bank of the Chandra, and the terrain is very similar to the previous day's. But now, the track begins to meander over the floodplain itself, which is a vast field of moraine broken only by huge mounds of the same material. We were told by our guide that this day's trek was much easier, involving a distance of only 13 km, and that we had to camp on the other side of another stream called Topkoyongma, or "the upper river". However, he assured us that this second stream was easily fordable during the day and that we could take it easy. We took him at his word, had many tea breaks on the way, and generally sauntered our way to the stream where a big surprise awaited us when we reached there at about 3:00 pm.

Topkoyongma was a monster! Its waters were a light shade of black due to the dissolved detritus of the glacier from which it was born. Roaring its way down a deep valley on the right, it was at least 30 metres wide; so furious was the speed of its waters that it created troughs and waves that were up to four feet deep and high. It carried unseen boulders along its bed—we could distinctly hear the booming, grating sound as they rolled along on the bed of the stream, like a series of explosions. To even think of crossing it in its present stage was sheer madness. But our position, because of wrong information, was critical. What had happened was that our mules and porters had not tarried on the hike from Topkogongma (like we did) and had crossed Topkoyongma by 11:00 am when it had not yet become the raging torrent it was now. All our supplies and gear—tents, sleeping bags, food, stoves, heavy jackets, torches—were now on the other side of the stream whereas we were stranded on the nearer side for

the night! Food was not the critical item, but the tents and sleeping bags certainly were. With night temperatures here dropping to zero, spending a night in the open was fraught with grave consequences. We were, therefore, desperate enough to allow our guide, Somdev from the mountaineering institute in Manali, to attempt to cross the stream after tying a safety line.

Somdev could go only about 10 feet into the foaming waters before he lost his footing and had to be quickly pulled back to the bank. By now it was 4:00 pm and we knew we had only about 90 minutes of sunlight left to come up with something. The spot was, if anything, even bleaker and more inhospitable than Topkogongma. Constituted entirely of boulders and rocks, the place offered no shelter from the elements. We looked around for a cave or a *dogri* such as the type used by shepherds but could find none—no shepherd ventures this far up into these grassless regions. We decided to rig a line across the river and see if one of us could cross it; if this worked then the porters (who by now had no doubt reached the day's campsite) could be called back and the supplies and equipment winched back on the same line. Ankit, a lecturer in the college at Kullu, and Ram Singh, one of the porters unlucky enough to be stranded with us, volunteered for this dangerous assignment. The rope was strung across the stream without much difficulty, but it had an ominous lag in the middle where the torrent was most frightening! The slack would not go away no matter how hard we tried to tighten the rope. Ram Singh latched himself to the rope with a safety line attached, grasped it with his hands and legs, upside down, and crawled hand over foot, inch by inch, till he reached the bottom of the lag—at this point he was almost completely immersed in the raging waters. He had to be dragged back by the safety line. It became obvious that the rope had to be rigged at a higher level, but we couldn't go too high above the stream either since the rope was not long enough!

It took us half an hour to re-locate the line; Ram Singh went across on the first attempt this time, albeit thoroughly soaked. Ankit went next and our manoeuvre had been a success. In no time at all the tents, sleeping bags, a stove, and ready-to-eat food was winched across. The rocky and precipitous banks of the Topkoyongma offered no tenting sites but we had to make do with whatever was available, clearing rocks and stones, and be content if we managed to pitch our tents even at a 10-degree gradient! It was a cold, uncomfortable night with four persons to a two-man tent, the stove stopped working before all the food could be cooked, and continuous icy winds were blowing down from the glaciers, funnelling into the Yongma valley and straight into our tents! But we all knew it could have been much worse and were therefore not too disheartened.

However, we had learnt our lesson and were up and packed by five the next morning, happy to be doing something other than freezing on top of each other in the tents! The Topkoyongma was now unrecognisable—gone was the roaring sound of the previous evening, the furious waves, and even its colour had become much lighter. It was now a quiet, gentle stream, barely knee high, and we were able to ford it with ease. Our guide later informed us that though the stream was notoriously unpredictable and had claimed a number of lives in the past (people who misjudged the depth as well as the strength of the current), and although he had been on this trek a number of times over the last 10 years, he had never seen the stream so swollen with water or so dark in colour. The only possible explanation for this development is that with increasing day temperatures, the snowmelt is getting accelerated— not a good omen at all for the future. This also means, however, that the old and accepted itinerary for this trek should change: the night halt at Topkogongma on the second day should be beyond the stream and not before it, which would entail leaving Chandratal very early. Perhaps a better option will be to leave the second day's schedule as it is, and to leave Topkogongma earlier, at about 5:00 am, make almost a forced march so as to reach Topkoyongma latest by 11:00 am, and cross it before it becomes a torrent.

The need for this change becomes all the more apparent and desirable when one reaches the actual campsite, i.e. the spot where we would have camped had we not been stranded on the other side of the stream. It is barely a kilometre from the Yongma: after one climbs out of the steep valley of the stream, one walks across a green and level pasture, with the Chandra on one's left, till a promontory which juts out into the river valley is reached, about 100 feet above the river. This is the camping site, and I have seen few better ones. To the west is the Chandra, flowing sedately, now an infant; to the north are the imposing and snow-covered Mulkila and Baralacha ranges where the Chandra is born; to the east are pastures rising gently to much lower, rounded ridgetops; to the south (behind us) is the convoluted valley of the Chandra, descending towards Chandratal. The sheer vastness of the landscape and the spread of the canvas is unbelievable. The scene is particularly magnificent early in the morning when the sun rises from behind the low ridges on the east, colouring all the peaks to the north and north-west with a golden hue. One can actually see this golden shade moving down the mountains, like a huge, celestial searchlight, lighting up the whole landscape till it reaches the Chandra itself, turning it instantaneously into a blinding ribbon of molten gold. This is the true no-man's-land: no government exists here, nobody lives here, and no shepherd visits here due to the risks involved in crossing the two *topkos*. This is truly the paradise every high-altitude trekker dreams of. How we all wished that we could spend a night here, the night that circumstances had robbed us of. But unfortunately our schedule could not be altered because of downstream (or, in our case, upstream!) arrangements, and we could spend only a couple of hours here. However, all of us swore that we shall come back here one day, from the Baralacha side this time, and spend at least a couple of days in this pasture that even the Gaddi forgot.

The campsite is quite big and can easily accommodate 20 tents. A little spring meanders through one side of the site so fresh water is available in abundance. After the previous night's sparse dinner we now breakfasted like kings, especially as this was the final day of the trek and there was no need to hoard our food supplies. Keeping us company were a couple of choughs and a wagtail, quite fearless in their isolation. What was disappointing, however, was the litter and rubbish lying around: chicken feathers, plastic bags, tin cans, cardboard boxes, and signs of extinguished campfires everywhere; this when barely a hundred people make this trek each year. We spent an hour clearing the rubbish and burning what we could, and packed up the rest to take back to the civilisation from where it had originated in the first place. But this raises an important issue which the Himachal government, especially its tourism and forest departments, would do well to confront. The state has scores of the most wonderful treks, and more and more of them are now attracting trekkers from all parts of the country and the world. The government too has now started promoting this as an adventure sport, but it is doing absolutely nothing to provide some minimum but basic facilities on these trails to counter the environmental impact of large numbers of people traversing them every year. The trails should be left as they are; in fact, it would be disastrous if any attempts were to be made to make them "easier" or "safer" by building bridges or widening the tracks, etc. The true trekker is looking for a challenge, welcomes the difficulties associated with the sport, accepts the element of risk involved, and would like nature to be left alone. What is required, however, are certain interventions to ameliorate the impact on the environment, particularly at the campsites which are more or less fixed. The government should dig rubbish pits, provide a couple of pit latrines, and erect breast-high walls in the shape of a small square room (without a roof) where cooking can be done: just these simple steps would eliminate 95 per cent of the waste generated in the campsites, and preserve their cleanliness and beauty. All this requires minimal expenditure; all that is needed is some labour and local materials like stones. No amount of seminars in Shimla or road shows in Delhi can promote genuine and sustainable nature tourism if we allow our natural assets to be degraded, or do not take proactive steps to protect them.

With great reluctance we left the camp at about 11:00 am as we had to reach Baralacha Pass before sunset. Our direction was still due north-west, but now the Chandra valley spreads out considerably and takes the form of huge pastures, spotted with isolated patches of moraine.

In a pensive mood, viewing the Baralacha glacier—source of the Chandra River

It is a lovely walk over a succession of gently rounded ridges and the ascent is also very gradual. The day was bright and the sun positively hot. After about 90 minutes one crests a ridge and straight ahead, about a kilometre away, one can clearly see the Baralacha glacier. Two narrow streams of water can be seen descending from it, gradually fanning out to half a dozen dazzling ribbons—the Chandra River—adorning the neck of the mountain like a flowing pendant. Actually, it appears to be two glaciers in the shape of a "V", the two arms separated by a huge ridge or spur, but we were informed by Somdev that it was actually one huge glacier and the intervening ridge was also made of ice but covered by moraine. The glacier must have been at least two kilometres wide, and we could clearly see its snout and a black ice wall next to it. It is a magnificent view and one cannot but be humbled by this sight of one of the most fascinating processes of nature, the creation of water; a process we so unthinkingly take for granted each time we pull the flush in our urbanised tenements! Looking at the creation of this beautiful river I felt an immense respect for the forces of nature, but I felt also an overwhelming sadness which I could not explain: was it due to our lack of concern for these treasures of nature, so wrapped up are we in our consumerist materialism? Or was it due to a lurking fear that the days of these magnificent creations of nature are numbered, their future uncertain in the age of the hydrocarbon? Or was it the sadness of the poet who saw a beautiful flower bloom and die in the desert, unnoticed and unsung? I guess I'll never know, and perhaps I don't want to; the sense of sadness is in itself fulfilling.

At this point the track veers northwards, and after four days we left the Chandra behind us, heading instead to meet its sister, the Bhaga, at the Baralacha Pass. We walked over an almost flat plain for more than an hour, at the end of which we descended into a wide gulley through which flowed another stream, or *topko*, no one had told us about. Even our guide was surprised—another indication of how the changing climate is altering the landscape. This *topko* appeared to originate from the north-east, somewhere to the right of the Baralacha Pass: its waters were a dull but deep red, indicating that it was rain-fed and not snow-fed like the streams we had encountered over the last three days. Its waters were icy cold. Crossing this stream, we emerged from the gulley to find Baralacha Pass straight ahead, about four kilometres away. Using our binoculars we could even make out the trucks en route to the pass. The last two kilometres to the pass are over a huge elliptical depression which must have been a lake in times past. We reached Baralacha Pass (16,500 feet), where our vehicles were waiting, at 4:30 pm. On the pass, which is a desolate, windswept place, stands a shack festooned with coloured flags. Outside it is the inevitable cairn of stones that serves as a temple. In keeping with tradition we placed one stone each on the cairn, silently thanked the gods for the successful completion of our little adventure, and headed back towards Keylong, about 70 km away.

Baralacha Pass is on the Manali–Leh road, one of the many high mountain passes on this route. Driving back to Keylong, after about eight kilometres one comes across a small lake on the left of the road: this is Surajtal (the sun lake). It is an unfortunate little water body for it is too close to human presence, unlike Chandratal. Completely dammed on three sides, only a little water seeps through on the eastern side of the body, and the lake is rapidly shrinking in size due to the debris from road construction being dumped into it. What surprised us, however, was that no river or stream emerged from it. It is generally believed that the river Bhaga emanates from Surajtal. We found that this was not so: the Bhaga, from its point of origin, flows westwards, and the western end of Surajtal is blocked off by a huge wall of debris *Surajtal lake* and rocks and shale. In fact, the Bhaga originates about a kilometre

west of Surajtal in a small valley that is capped by a glacier. It then flows in a westerly-south-westerly direction till it meets the Chandra at a place called Tandi, just below Keylong. It flows westwards from there as the Chandrabhaga till it finally becomes the Chenab and flows into Pakistan. When we reached Tandi the next day we had completed a full circuit—followed one river to its source and descended from the source of the second to its confluence with the first. We had travelled from the moon to the sun.

2004

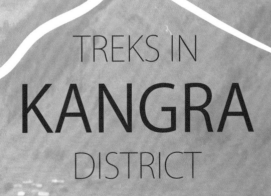

TREKS IN

KANGRA

DISTRICT

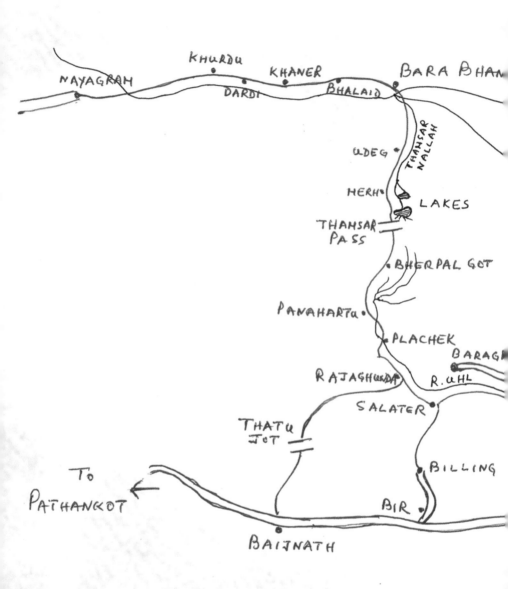

Chhota and Bara Bhangal

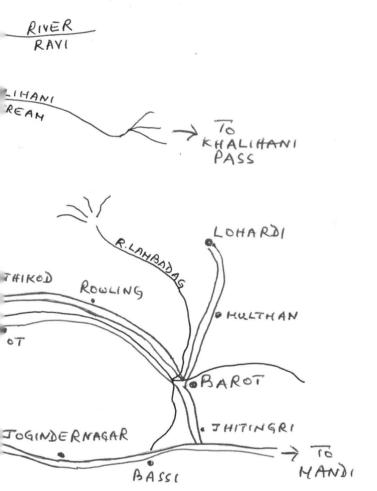

RIVER
RAVI

LIHANI
REAM

TO
KHALIHANI
PASS

R. LAHBADAS

LOHARDI

THIKOD

ROWLING

KULTHAN

OT

BAROT

JOGINDERNAGAR

JHITINGRI

TO
MANDI

BASSI

MAP NOT TO SCALE

Chhota Bhangal

*T*here remain only two landlocked tehsils in Himachal today—the Dodra Kwar valley in Shimla district, from which emerges the Rupin River on its way to join the Yamuna, and the Bara-Chhota Bhangal area of the Palampur subdivision of Kangra district, the catchment basin of the Uhl and Lambadug rivers. In a few years from now, and at the cost of a few thousand trees, the Dodra Kwar valley shall be linked to a road that is being constructed over the Chanshal Pass (13,000 feet), but sheer logistics should ensure that Bara-Chhota Bhangal remains a trekkers' paradise for some time to come. (The road from Larot to Dodra Kwar over the Chanshal Pass has since been constructed).

Though clubbed together in common parlance, Chhota Bhangal and Bara Bhangal are actually two separate valleys, divided by the massive Thamsar Pass (4,704 metres) of the Dhauladhar range. The area below the pass on the Baijnath side is Chhota Bhangal, and the area beyond it, bordering Chamba district, is Bara Bhangal; both fall in Kangra district. No one is exactly sure how this name came about: one version claims that the inhabitants of this area originally came from Bengal (it is an established fact that the erstwhile royal family of the neighbouring district of Mandi, the Sains, were from Bengal); another version has it that the area acquired its name from the word *bhangali*, meaning Adivasi or tribals. The area being talked about is vast, almost 1,500 sq. km, and very sparsely inhabited. Chhota Bhangal is accessed from a small village called Bir, about 12 km from the subdivisional headquarters of Jogindernagar on the Mandi–Pathankot national highway. Bir has become a prosperous and bustling centre for Tibetan crafts, and has a substantial population of Tibetans and monasteries. Situated at a height of 5,000 feet, surrounded by verdant green vegetation and a few tea gardens, its backdrop is formed by the 7,000-foot-high hills that guard the approaches to the valley of Chhota Bhangal. There is an old forest rest house at Bir with three bedrooms (attached toilets)—one can ask for no better base camp for a night halt. From Bir one proceeds to Billing, 14 km away, via a single-lane road that winds its way up 2,000 feet through some of the thickest oak and rhododendron forests one has ever seen. The local divisional forest officer informed us that the traditional usufruct rights over this forest were managed by a "mahila samiti", and these women would not allow any felling or lopping of trees in the forest— the primary reason behind its verdant richness. In fact, they had even imposed fines on those who dared to defy their diktat! All one can say is: strength to their elbows!

Billing is nothing but a broad expanse of pasture jutting out into the Baijnath valley, ending in a sheer precipice with the plains spread out 2,000 feet below. This natural feature makes it an ideal point for hang-gliding and paragliding. The sport had become immensely popular here a few years back, but a couple of accidents have set it back a bit. There is no reason, however, why it cannot be revived with a dedicated push by the state's tourism department. After all, there will always be the element of risk in an adventure sport—it would cease to be one without this risk. We met a few enterprising local youths who provide the transportation from Bir, all the equipment required for hang-gliding, and a 40-minute accompanied flight on a double harness for just 1,500 rupees. Value for money, certainly!

The first stage of the trek is from Billing to Rajgundha, a distance of 18 km. The route stretches along the remains and alignment of a jeep track that had been carved out in the early 1960s, but has now fallen into disuse. The reasons for its abandonment and neglect are not very clear (since all the hard effort and investment had already been put in), but probably lie in the extreme backwardness of the area and its political marginalisation. In any case, the road is no longer

jeepable but provides a gentle climb for the first six kilometres to a saddle on the escarpment that opens onto the valley of the Uhl River, flowing in a roughly North–South direction. This place is called Slater and consists of a solitary shack (dhaba) where one can get a fairly decent meal of hot rice, dal, and a vegetable curry the main ingredient of which has to be potato since they grow it here in extremely large quantities! The elevation here is about 8,000 feet and we had traversed through a very interesting gradation and profiling of vegetation en route—beginning with the pines at Billing one has passed through, in that order, oak (kharsu) mixed with rhododendron, then deodar, fir, and finally spruce.

Slater Pass is the entry point to Uhl valley and Chhota Bhangal proper. As one approaches it from Billing the river can be seen flowing far below, from left to right, in an approximately North–South alignment. The interesting feature is that the right bank of the river (where we were) is in Kangra district and the far left bank in Mandi district! Straight ahead and across the river rises a high ridge, beyond which is the valley of the mysterious sounding Lambadug. It too flows southwards and joins the Uhl about 17 km below at an enchanting little village called Barot. The left bank of the Uhl is far more developed than the right bank and has a number of villages strung along its length for a distance of about 20 km upstream, beginning from Barot—Rowling, Kothikod, Nalanta, and Baragram, each with about 40 houses. A non-metalled road has crawled its way up from Barot to Baragram and provides the lifeline so badly needed for the economic development of these areas, locked up in their own time warp for centuries. The land here grows exquisite disease-free potatoes, cabbages, radishes, and rajmash, which now, thanks to this road, find a ready market in Bir. The most visible symbols of this new connectivity, however, are the sparkling new tin roofs decking the houses. Just a few years ago these roofs would have been made of the traditional wooden planks, or rough-cut heavy slate tiles. But with wood getting scarcer and newer alternatives becoming available, the villagers have en masse switched over to the ubiquitous galvanised tin sheets that the new road has now made available to them. I have no doubt that in a

PAGES
212–213:
Confluence of
the Uhl (on
the right) and
Lambadug
rivers above
Barot
Courtesy:
Vaibhav
Rajour

few more years the characteristic stone houses of the Chhota Bhangal valley would have been replaced by cement and concrete structures, and modern civilisation would have firmly established itself in these beautiful vales. We would be slightly the poorer for this "progress".

One turns left at Slater and proceeds upstream on the right bank of the Uhl for about seven kilometres to the village of Rajgundha (8,700 feet). The valley here is much wider; the village consists of about 20 houses, and the government has also graciously left its imprint by establishing two offices here: the offices of the forest department block officer of Kothikod, and a farm of the agriculture department. The latter grows seed potatoes for further distribution to the farmers in the state—the cold, disease-free environment here provides ideal conditions for this crop. Other vegetables are also grown by the villagers here, but since they are not as fortunate as their brethren on the left bank in having a motorable road, the economic returns are not so good. The most welcome news for the trekker, however, is the fact that Rajgundha also has a forest inspection hut with electricity and running water, supplied by a *kuhal* or natural water channel flowing next to it. Cooking facilities are available in an adjoining outhouse. The accommodation is more than adequate: one small bedroom and one big living room, which can hold six to eight persons in sleeping bags quite comfortably. Interestingly, the entire Chhota-Bara Bhangal area is a declared wildlife sanctuary known as the Dhauladhar Sanctuary.

From Rajgundha one gets the first good view of Thamsar Pass, about 30 km away looking straight up the valley. It is a formidable sight from here, the pass stretching like a rampart at 4,704 metres (roughly 6,000 feet higher than our elevation at Rajgundha). Apart from guarding the access to Bara Bhangal, which lies beyond it, the pass also is the source of the Uhl River, born of its snows and the run-offs from its attendant features—the Sijotru Dhar and the Thamsar Jot. Rajgundha, with its fairly comfortable accommodation, is an ideal base camp for a portfolio of treks. The big one, and the most difficult, of course, is the trek over Thamsar Pass and into Bara Bhangal. It takes two days: proceeding from Rajgundha one crosses the last hamlet in this valley just a kilometre later, a forlorn group of 10 houses called Kukurgunda. One continues upstream on the right bank of the Uhl for another 10 km, climbing almost unnoticeably till Plachek where the track crosses over to the left bank. There used to be a *pucca* bridge here, but it was washed away in a furious flash flood in the July of 2001. The torrent also destroyed the only tea shop and claimed one life. The forest department has now constructed a temporary wooden bridge, and the tea shop owner is back in business in a reconstructed shack. There is also a two-roomed building here that used to serve as an inspection hut of the forest department, but is now in a dilapidated and unusable state. However, realising the strategic importance of this building (it is the only permanent structure between Rajgundha and Bara Bhangal), the deputy commissioner of Kangra has sanctioned funds for its restoration. Repair of the hut shall be a big help for travellers on this route, which experiences fairly heavy "traffic".

Bara Bhangal village, located on the other side of the pass, has a population of about 600. Their entire requirement of food grains and other necessities has to be brought up from Bir by mules between the end of May and mid-October, the period when the pass is open. Furthermore, the residents of Bara Bhangal are primarily graziers and shepherds since the opportunity for agriculture is extremely limited in these harsh climes. By November, they start moving down with their flocks along this same route, down to the Kangra valley and even beyond to Punjab where they have traditional grazing rights, and even own lands and houses. These twice a year migrations are a nightmare for the forest department because the flocks of sheep cause immense damage to the forests, especially to the new plantations. By one estimate there are more than two lakh sheep making this journey. During British times, and even until about 15 years ago, the department used to establish barriers all along the migration route to check the numbers and to ensure that the sheep stuck to the routes demarcated for the purpose. However, this has been done away with by successive governments purely for populist reasons. In addition, the graziers are expert poachers and exact a heavy toll on the wildlife— the area remains a sanctuary more or less only on paper.

The first day's halt is at a place called Panihartu Got (3,574 metres), a stony and bleak, windswept waste with a couple of rough stone huts providing a kind of community shelter, unless one has one's own tents. On the second day one has to cross the Thamsar Pass and this should be done positively before noon, so the start has to be early—at about 5:00 am as it is a steep, five-hour climb to the feature. There can be some snow on either side of the pass even as late as September-end, but this can be easily negotiated with a little bit of caution. (The best period to cross Thamsar Pass is between mid-July and mid-September. We attempted it in mid-October and had to return from below Panihartu because of fresh snowfalls). On the other side is the catchment area of river Ravi, flowing down to Chamba, and in which is located the legendary and mysterious village of Bara Bhangal (8,500 feet), the very mention of which can freeze the heart of a government employee such is the fear of a posting to this place! It is advisable to rest at Bara Bhangal for a couple of days before starting on the return trip. Fortunately, there is a forest hut here too, or one can always take accommodation in one of the village houses. There are a number of route options for the return journey: one can either return the way one came; or exit via the Jalsu Pass to Baijnath; or follow the course of the Ravi to Holi in Chamba district; or cross the Kalihani Pass into Kullu district, emerging at Patlikuhal, halfway between Kullu and Manali. The first three options are the easiest (though there is a fairly alarming one-kilometre stretch in the gorge of the Ravi en route to Holi), each requiring about two days. The most challenging route, however, is the trek across the Kalihani, which takes four days: this is because even though the Kalihani Pass is the same height as the Thamsar, it is more towards the north and therefore more snow-bound, making it that much more difficult to negotiate.

For the trekker who just loves walking or climbing the mountains without exposing himself to too much risk or exertion, there are a number of options available from the same base at Rajgundha. Immediately behind the forest rest house is a steep ridge, scaling which involves a continuous ascent of two hours to a pass called

Temple of local deity on the saddle of Thati Jot the Thati Jot (10,500 feet)—though steep, the trek is pleasant as the trail wanders through dense *kail* (blue pine), fir, and spruce forests. Perched on the saddle of the pass is a small temple with an idol of the local deity placed in it. We were quite puzzled to see bangles, ribbons, and other feminine trinkets placed before the deity. Soon a group of young girls appeared, picked up the offerings, and went on their way! Our guide revealed to us that it was a custom here for married women to leave these trinkets in the temple for unmarried girls, and both were blessed by the transaction!

Thati Pass overlooks the Baijnath and Sansar valleys on the west, and one can clearly see the town of Baijnath spread out below, about 10 km away by a bridle path that meanders through the forested slopes on the other side. This is an extremely popular route for people travelling from Baijnath to Chhota Bhangal; the journey takes about four hours on foot. The alternative—from Baijnath to Bir by bus, then on foot to

Billing, Slater, and on to any of the villages in the Uhl valley—would be far more expensive and time consuming. Also, most Chhota Bhangal villagers own lands and houses in the Baijnath and Sansar valleys since they migrate to these places for the winters. Traffic on this route is, therefore, fairly heavy and there is a constant coming and going over the pass, especially of school children (who have to perforce study in Baijnath) visiting their parents and relatives in Chhota Bhangal.

A second, fairly easy but longer trek is from Rajgundha to Barot, traversing down the Uhl valley. From the rest house one goes back about six kilometres to Slater Pass the way one had come. At the pass, however, instead of turning right (west) towards Billing, one turns left (south-east), descending about 500 feet to just above the Uhl River through dense undergrowth, blue pine, and oak. The path is little more than a goat track now, falling into disuse after a motorable road was constructed on the opposite (left) bank of the river. Laid out in neat spacing on the opposite bank are the little hamlets of Rowling, Kothikod, and Baragram, sparkling in the pure mountain sunlight. But, leaving Slater Pass one is caught in a strange geopolitical twist—where earlier the right bank was in Kangra district, it is now in Mandi, and the

A view of Baragram village from across the Uhl River

left bank of the river is now in Kangra! There is only one village of any consequence on the right bank between Slater and Barot, or in fact between Rajgundha and Barot, known as Mayot, about six kilometres from Slater. It is a big settlement with about 100 houses, and is fairly well-developed with cemented pathways, a drainage system, a big middle school, a water supply scheme, etc. Some of the houses were really captivating—made of pure deodar (cedar) sleepers, no doubt obtained through the timber distribution rights system (whereby a villager gets two trees every five years for his bona fide personal use for about five rupees each where the market price of these trees may be about rupees fifty or sixty thousand each!). Each house we saw could not have needed less than 20 or 30 trees, and would cost a fortune if transplanted into any urban environment. Such, however, is the politics of the day that even though this pernicious practice of TD rights (as this system is called) involves the extraction of 1,25,000 cubic metres of prime timber from Himachal's forests each year, and is one of the primary causes for the degradation of its quality forests, no political party is even willing to talk about revoking, or even rationalising, this anachronism. (In 2009, the Himachal High Court compelled the government to drastically restrict this right to a limited number of people).

The distance from Mayot to Barot is about six kilometres via a track that hugs the fast-flowing Uhl, about 200 feet above the river level. It initially meanders through empty agricultural fields and grasslands, hugging the contours of the hill, with towering forests of blue pine and deodar dominating the ridgeline. After about three kilometres the track widens into a rough road that is being built from the Barot side, presently suitable only for tractors. The road descends almost to river-level, and the walk from here to Barot is extremely pleasant and enjoyable, canopied under a thick growth of alnus and pine with the river happily gurgling along on the left. Barot itself is a delightful little village, and it is here that the Uhl converges with the mysterious Lambadug coming silently and unnoticed from the north-east. Barot is famous for being the location of the first hydel project commissioned in northern India in the 1930s—the Shanan Power House. The design

of the project itself is amazingly simple: the waters of the Uhl are diverted through a small barrage and dropped to a place called Bassi (near Jogindernagar) a few thousand feet below via huge surface pipes or the penstock. The head so created is adequate to generate 110 MW of power at the power station at Bassi. The British had laid a railway line from Pathankot to Jogindernagar to transport the heavy machinery and materials needed for the project. The most amazing thing is that since there were no roads to Barot at the time, the entire equipment, materials, and supplies required for construction of the project was carried up on trollies. A trolley track was laid by British engineers from Bassi to Barot, climbing straight up 4,000 feet along gradients unimaginable even by today's technological standards! The trolley is winched up in stage and the track is dotted with successive winch stations. The system remains operational even today, though its utility has considerably

Balancing reservoir of the Shanan HEP at Barot
Courtesy: Vaibhav Rajour

The famous log hut at Barot. Unfortunately, a concrete monstrosity has now come up next to it

reduced now that a road has been constructed to Barot. But a ride on the trolley is still possible with the right connections and it simply is the most thrilling experience imaginable, cresting one ridge after another, through forests and pastures, with panoramic landscapes unfolding themselves in never-ending succession. The little village itself is built around the project—a few shops, two rest houses (a log hut of the PWD and the project rest house. Both of them are delightful places ideal for the tourist, but advance booking is recommended). In recent years the Shanan Project has become a bone of contention between the Himachal and Punjab state governments. Surprisingly, the project is the property of the latter even though it is located well within the former's territory! For some strange reason it was not transferred to Himachal when the state was carved out of Punjab in the early 1960s. It today constitutes a Punjabi enclave within Himachal, which is an oddity and an anachronism to say the least. Choosing to remain quiet earlier, the Himachal government has of late begun to demand that the project be transferred to the state to correct this historical anomaly, but Punjab will have nothing of it. One suspects that Punjab's response is dictated not so much by the possibility of losing 110 MW of power but more by the prospect of losing its rights to the 5-star guest house constructed with the project at this beautiful hill station! The Shanan guest house is a much sought-after holiday accommodation among the bureaucrats and politicians at Chandigarh, and they will not let it go without a struggle. Barot also has a trout breeding farm of the fisheries department where fingerlings are allowed to grow before they are released into the mountain streams. This is worthwhile work being done as most streams in the state where this fish was found in abundance just a few years ago—Tirthan, Sainj, Andhra, Lambadug, Uhl, upper reaches of the Ravi, Parbati, etc.—have been so mercilessly poached, dynamited, and silted (by construction activities) that this culinary delight has all but disappeared. A few private breeders have also established such farms, mainly in the Kullu district, and are selling the fish in Delhi and Chandigarh at 200 to 250 rupees per kilo.

With its calm and tranquil atmosphere, Barot is the ideal place to terminate one's trek from the Chhota Bhangal area. However, it also serves as a hub from where other treks originate. For example, if one goes upstream on the Lambadug from Barot, one crosses the small village of Multan and reaches Lohardi, the last settlement on this road, after about 10 km. To the right is a high ridge crossed via the Sari Pass (about 10,000 feet), beyond which lies the Lug valley of Kullu district—a fairly easy trek that takes two days. If one crosses the river to its left bank at Lohardi, one proceeds on foot for five kilometres to Poling, the last village in this valley. Straight in front, stretched out in all its massive grandeur, are the formidable ramparts that guard the Bara Bhangal region. As one looks straight up and to the left, on the massif is Narlu Pass that spans across the ridge between the Uhl and Lambadug valleys, and brings one to Rajgundha (where we had camped for three days). To the right and at a much greater height are the Lolar alpine pastures, and beyond them lies Makori Pass, which leads on to

Bara Bhangal. The shepherds of Bara Bhangal who wish to go to Kangra district travel by the Thamsar Pass, while those who wish to go towards Kullu or Mandi districts prefer to use the Makori Pass.

One exits Barot by taking the motorable road, which winds downwards for 20 km and joins the Mandi–Pathankot highway near Jogindernagar. Just prior to this junction one passes through a tiny hamlet called Jhatingri. Its claim to fame are the ruins of a palace of the raja of Mandi, constructed as a hunting lodge cum romantic getaway. It was acquired by the state government some years ago in dubious circumstances, allegedly to benefit the raja's heirs. Since then the government has been wondering what to do with it! It has since been transferred to the state tourism corporation, which is looking for some private investor to take it over and build a hotel on it. The site is amazingly attractive, completely surrounded by dense forests, but the downside is its location (too far from the railhead at Pathankot). Hopefully some day a bright entrepreneur will come up with a plan to develop this otherwise idyllic property.

2002

Looking up the Lambadug valley towards Lohardi village
Courtesy: Vaibhav Rajour

Bara Bhangal
THE FORGOTTEN VALLEY

Bara Bhangal is a fairly large village situated deep inside Ravi valley in the extreme north of Kangra district. It is also the name given to the entire area located between the Dhauladhar and Manimahesh ranges in the district. Accessed by extremely difficult and high passes located to its south, east, and north from Kangra, Kullu, and Chamba (Bharmour subdivision) districts respectively, the only route into it via a valley is from the western side, and this is the Ravi valley itself. The river bisects Bara Bhangal in half as it flows from east to west, exiting at Nayagram, again in the Bharmour subdivision of Chamba. There is a track along the entirety of this valley (it is actually a deep, precipitous gorge) from Nayagram to Bara Bhangal, but, as we were to discover, this route is no less dangerous or difficult than any of the passes. Bara Bhangal is the only major landlocked valley left in Himachal, now that Dodra Kwar has been connected to the rest of Shimla district by a motorable road over the 13,000-foot Chanshal Pass. The region has been accorded the status of a protected area and declared as the Dhauladhar Wildlife Sanctuary. In the normal course one would expect these unique features to attract trekkers like a magnet—this has not happened, primarily because the area is so remote that the sheer logistics prove insurmountable. Another reason being that very little is known about this valley and even the government has given it a go-by, as we were to discover ourselves.

The route most commonly taken by the residents of Bara Bhangal for entering and exiting the valley is the southern one, over the 17,500-foot Thamsar Jot or Pass, as most of the villagers have their relations

and own lands in the Bir/Billing area south of Thamsar, and also *The deep* because this is the only route on which mules can move. I had attempted *gorge of the* this trek for the first time in 2002 but had to return from just below *Ravi. The* *track to* the pass because of a sudden change in the weather. But in September *Nayagram* of 2003 we decided to try again. The trek from the roadhead at Bir on *can be seen on* the main Mandi–Palampur highway takes six days if one exits from *the right* the west via the Ravi valley, and eight days if one wishes to return the same way over the Thamsar. Since one of the joys of trekking is the exploration of new areas and encountering new challenges, we decided to take the Ravi route on the return leg. Up to Rajgundha/Plachek the route is the same as for Chhota Bhangal (described in the previous section), but once one crosses the Uhl at Plachek onto its left bank the real trek begins. One turns north from this point and suddenly the whole prospect changes: the landscape becomes grimmer, the trees start giving way to grasses and shrubs, the wind acquires an icy edge,

and the valley of the Uhl contracts into a canyon where sunlight peeps in with difficulty. It is hard to put into words and even more difficult to explain, but in the shadow of the mighty Thamsar there is something of a sense of foreboding, of being completely at the mercy of the elements. One feels puny and helpless.

It is about 16 km from Rajgundha (8,000 feet) to Panihartu (12,000 feet) via Plachek (9,000 feet), the second stage of which is much more strenuous. Located on the right bank of the Uhl, Panihartu is the campsite for the second day (Billing to Rajgundha having been the first day's trek); one has to cross an ice bridge over the Uhl to reach there, even as late as the middle of September. Three streams converge at this place, all fed by glaciers of the Thamsar massif, and merge to form the Uhl. Panihartu is one of the most desolate places I have ever seen: perched precariously on the slopes above the river, it is reached by a slipping-sliding climb of 100 metres from the river bank. There are no trees at this altitude and hence no shelter or firewood. There are no houses or huts here either as the village remains uninhabited for most part of the year. During the season between June and the beginning of September, when the pass is open and people travel on this route, some traders put up tents and provide a very rudimentary form of board and lodging to these itinerants. But when we reached there on the 11th of September, these hardy businessmen had already left for the winters. We were lucky enough, however, to find one huge tent made of a couple of tarpaulins still standing; apparently its owner had gone down with all his goods and was to return to take away the tent on his second trip. With a silent blessing for our unknown benefactor we moved into his tent for the night. It rained throughout the night, the cold was intense, and we could barely sleep, apprehensive that if the weather continued like this our second attempt at Thamsar too would be doomed.

We awoke on the third day at 5:00 am to be greeted by an enveloping mist through which a heavy drizzle was falling steadily. The mountains around us were concealed behind thick clouds. We gloomily surveyed this depressing scenario over a cup of tea, and when there was no let-up in the weather even after an hour, it looked like we would have to abort our attempt. However, there was one young couple from Bara Bhangal who had also camped at Panihartu for the night, on their way back after attending a family function at Baijnath. Suddenly, they shouldered their rucksacks and set off for the climb to the pass, telling us encouragingly that the weather would be better at the pass itself. We watched them climb for half an hour and were emboldened to follow when they showed no signs of turning back; after all, we reasoned, no one knew the conditions at Thamsar better than the locals of that valley. Within minutes camp was broken, the mules were loaded, and we set off at about 7:30 am without bothering about the luxury of a breakfast. It takes about four hours of strenuous climbing to attain Thamsar. One has to cross two steep ridges and reach a flattish ground interspersed with moraine and patches of grass. This is Bherpal Got or, literally, shepherd's ground, and is so named because shepherds camp here both while ascending to, or descending from, the pass. To the right of the track is a small ice field from which a little stream emerges and flows down to Panihartu. The rain had by now turned into a fine drizzle of sleet, and icy winds from the pass made it cut into our faces, which soon turned numb. We were by now thoroughly soaked and wondered whether we had made the right decision. At this point there was a sudden break in the clouds

The ramparts of Thamsar Pass

Glacier on Thamsar Pass

and we could now see the Thamsar in its full, dreaded majesty. It was about a kilometre (and an hour) away, towering about 250 metres over us. Its features were extremely unusual; it looked like the rampart of an ancient fort, a long line of crags and serrated peaks almost half a kilometre long. To reach it we had to traverse a big, slightly sloping field of rocks and boulders, climb an almost vertical shale slope, which was obviously the result of constant erosion of the crags on the pass, and all of a sudden we were on the Thamsar! On the other, northern side was Chamba district. As if to welcome us, the sun broke through the clouds, illuminating a small stone shrine festooned with red flags on the pass.

It was far too cold for us to tarry on the pass, much as we would have liked to; so after placing the obligatory stone on a cairn, we moved on. We could not help but notice, however, that the entire ridgeline was dotted with dozens of similar cairns, adding to the rampart-like appearance of the ridge on which the pass is situated. Looking north from the pass towards Bara Bhangal, one is amazed at the contrast between its two faces. There is nothing attractive or imposing about the southern aspect, which we had just traversed, but the view to the north is awe-inspiring: spread out at our feet, so to speak, were a succession of massive glaciers and snowfields, almost as far as the eye could see on all sides. We climbed down onto the first ice field as there was no way around it; it was a kilometre across and took us 45 minutes to cross. Fortunately, it was hard, compacted ice, and had no crevasses, but it was sloping away from the pass at a pronounced angle and finding one's grip on it with our ordinary trekking shoes was not easy at all. It had little trickles of water running over its surface from the sun melt and these had carved out thin, tendril-like grooves on its surface. Slipping and falling intermittently, we made it across the ice field to find that below us was spread out a huge lake, created by the melt from this and other glaciers around the pass. This lake has been the watery grave of many an unfortunate mule which, having lost its footing on the glaciers or the ice field, can only helplessly *Another* slide down the ice into its waters. The lake was huge! It must have been *view of the massive glacier* at least a kilometre wide and two kilometres long on its North–South *on Thamsar* axis—as big as Chandratal. Towards its northern end the valley walls on *Pass*

either side close in and through the opening gushes a violent torrent of water, the Thamsar Nullah as it is known, which joins the Ravi at the village of Bara Bhangal.

We skirted the lake on its western flank for about three kilometres, walking at times barely a foot above the clear, shimmering waters of the lake, and entered the valley of Thamsar Nullah. The track now follows this narrow valley, more of a gorge actually, all the way to the village of Bara Bhangal. By now the sleet had reverted to a fine rain; the cold was intense and the rain had made the narrow track very slippery, especially for the mules, making our progress extremely slow and risky. There are a number of rockfalls that have to be negotiated with great care. Six kilometres from the pass the valley broadens out and the stream forms another, much smaller lake known simply as the Dal. Below this is the campsite of Merh in the midst of a large meadow. It was completely deserted and desolate at this time, but in the summer months a few

Campsite at Udeg

tents do spring up here offering food and lodging. Merh is at 14,000 feet and is the natural base camp for those climbing to the pass from the Bara Bhangal side as, with an early start from here, one can cross the pass in about three hours and reach Plachek or even Rajgundha the next day. But for those descending from the pass, especially as late in the year as we were, it was too cold to camp, and it is advisable to push on further to Udeg, another eight kilometres down. The track from here to Udeg is at a constant gradient, descending to 12,000 feet over a distance of eight kilometres, but is treacherous at certain points. The Dal flows into two smaller lakes, from which a small stream emerges to join the larger Thamsar Nullah. The track is initially on the left bank but crosses over to the right bank a couple of kilometres below Merh.

Udeg has a fairly level camping ground next to the stream; in the summers the trekker can be sure of finding food and lodgings in the few tents that spring up here. However, only one was available when we reached, owned by one Vikram Kapoor of Palampur. He had initially planned to leave on this day but had been alerted of our arrival by the young couple who had left Panihartu before us, and in the spirit of generous hospitality and concern, which is so typical of the residents of these remote mountain regions, he had decided to stay back for another day. On enquiring about the young couple, Vikram informed us that they had passed through about three hours before us and should be reaching Bara Bhangal soon (it was about 5:00 pm then). They are brisk walkers these mountain people, and their secret lies not so much in their fitness levels (it is common to see them smoking *beedis* even while climbing!) as in their sure-footedness. I have been observing their style and method of walking on mountain tracks for a number of years to try and discover how they are so sure of foot in their plastic or rubber shoes, and even sandals, while we slither about in our Caterpillars and Woodlands! I believe the explanation lies in the fact that they take smaller steps so as not to stretch their muscles too much, and let their feet stay on the ground for only a fraction of a second so that their body weight is quickly transferred and the feet do not have time to slip or slide. We, on the other hand, concerned with finding a good grip at

each step, put all our weight on the advancing foot, try to find traction and, more often than not, start slipping on the bad tracks. We also tend to take longer strides, which upsets the natural balance of our bodies while climbing or descending. Our perpetual anxiety over slipping and falling doesn't help either. The most penetrating advice on this subject was given to me by a guide on one of my treks: "Sahib, you should treat the track as your enemy and attack it. If you give it too much respect it will overpower you!" Could anyone have put it any better?

Vikram Kapoor (our innkeeper for the night, as it were) is also a muleteer, and this is perhaps as good a time as any to talk about the mules and muleteers of Bara Bhangal. The hardy mule is the backbone of the economy of Bara Bhangal; without it life here would just not be possible and would revert to the Stone Age. Just about everything from the outside world is brought in on the backs of these splendid animals—food grains, building materials, farming implements, clothes, utensils, kerosene, etc. The state government sends in about 1,200 quintals of wheat and rice each year on mules to feed the public distribution system. Whatever little Bara Bhangal exports is also carried out by these mules. As such this is big business for people like Vikram: a mule here usually carries about 40 to 50 kilos of load and takes 9 to 10 days to make the round trip over Thamsar Pass (the other routes into Bara Bhangal are too difficult for mules to ply on them)—four days in, a couple of days' rest, and then another four days out. The charge for each mule is between 800 and 1,000 rupees. One train would typically consist of four to five animals, so a round trip would be worth about 4,000 or 5,000 rupees to the muleteer. But business is available for only four or five months in a year, and it is a tough way to make a living. It is also extremely risky; every year a number of mules die on the glaciers or slip off the narrow trails—we saw two carcasses just below the glacier. No bank will insure these animals, and the death of even one can mean ruination for its poor owner. The shocking thing is that successive state governments have done nothing to either improve the track from Plachek to Bara Bhangal, or create an insurance scheme for the mules. Hundreds of crores are spent (and siphoned off) on national and state highways so that tourists can holiday in Shimla, but not a rupee is spent on a track which is the lifeline for 600 people, a track so difficult and risky that people perish on it, and one which even the very old, young, and sick have to use due to the lack of other options. Granted that this track can never be made motorable, and granted also that there are stretches of it (for example, over the glaciers and the approach to the pass) about which nothing can be done, but the other portions can be widened, the gradients improved, and the rock faces blasted so as to make them less dangerous for both man and mules. Similarly, means of transport being limited to the mule and employment opportunities in Bara Bhangal being zero, the authorities should have realised the vital role played by the muleteers in both these sectors and should at least have evolved an insurance scheme for them by now. The government has failed miserably in creating any employment opportunities in this inaccessible region; the least it could do is protect the means of employment created by these hardy people themselves. One is saddened by the distortion in priorities of even democratic governments.

It had stopped raining by now and the evening sun was out. Not very bright or warming at this time, it nonetheless held the promise of a warm and cheerful day on the morrow. We spent the night in Vikram's capacious tent, about 12 of us and two goats. The far end of the tent was the cooking area; since we were almost at the treeline, a small quantity of firewood was available. Smoke from the fire almost asphyxiated us, but at least it kept the interior warm. We had hot dal and chapatis for dinner that night and, after the frugal regime at Panihartu, enjoyed every morsel. The mules spent the night grazing out in the meadow—two of them strayed far away, as they are wont to do. It took our poor muleteer two extra hours the next morning to round them up.

The morning of our fourth day was straight out of a refrigerator: crisp, dry, and cold. Walled in by the valley sides on the east and west, we could see a succession of magnificent peaks to the north, covered with snow and dazzling in the rays of the morning sun. Beyond them,

we were told, lay the famous Manimahesh Lake, below Kailash Parbat. There is also a trek from Bara Bhangal to Manimahesh, but it is so arduous that usually only shepherds and some hardy locals attempt it. The acceptable trek to this lake, of course, is from Hadsar in Bharmour subdivision of Chamba district. We took it easy and tarried since the weather was good and it is only five kilometres to Bara Bhangal from Udeg, which takes about two and a half hours. We spent some time with our binoculars, trying to spot the ghoral or Himalayan tahr on the slopes and crags above us: these species of mountain goats abound at these heights and can usually be spotted early in the morning. When the sun hits the higher reaches they come out to graze in the warmth of the sun's rays. But we saw none, possibly because ours was a fairly well-travelled route and these shy animals must have learnt to avoid these corridors. We finally bid farewell to Vikram and left Udeg at 8:30 am. The descent from Udeg is quite steep as the track descends from 12,000 feet to 8,500 feet (altitude of the village of Bara Bhangal) over a distance of only five kilometres. Initially on the right bank of the Thamsar stream, after about two kilometres the track crosses back to the left bank over a couple of wooden logs. The Ravi meets the Thamsar Nullah almost at right angles five kilometres from Udeg— while the former flows from east to west, the latter flows from south to north. One can see the village of Bara Bhangal from about an hour away, located on the far, or northern, side of the Ravi just above the confluence of the two rivers. But to reach there one has to negotiate a steep descent, ford the Thamsar stream, and cross a second nullah coming from the south-east. This is the Kalihani stream descending from the Kalihani Pass, beyond which lies Kullu district. There is an interesting, three-day trekking route from Bara Bhangal to Patlikuhal in the Beas valley over the pass. Used only by the occasional trekkers and Gaddis, the Kalihani Pass is lower than Thamsar but is reported to have more snow on it. The Kalihani Nullah joins the Thamsar at this point and, barely a hundred metres on, their waters debouch into the bigger Ravi. We crossed the Ravi about 500 metres beyond this point over a heavy log bridge, which must have been a fine structure at one time but successive floods had washed away some of the logs, weakened the others, and severely damaged parts of the abutments. The bridge was now in a precarious state and would not be able to withstand the next major flood in the river. Once again, the apathy of the government was exposed: no attempt had been made to repair or replace this bridge even though it is the only link these villagers have with the rest of the world.

Bara Bhangal is a very large village consisting of about 60 houses with a population of approximately 600. The village is divided in half, and stretches along the right bank of the Ravi for about half a kilometre, dominated by massive bluffs on its northern aspect. There is an impressive grove of deodar trees at its western end, which is a flat plateau rising sheer from the Ravi. The forest department had, in 2003 itself, constructed a simple but functional rest house in the middle of this grove. Not many officers come on tour to this place, for obvious

The forest department's rest house at Bara Bhangal

reasons, but nonetheless the rest house meets a much felt need and the occasional trekker also benefits: our party was the first to reside in it and we are proud of the fact that ours are the first names in the rest house register! Built entirely of wood and other local materials, the building has been designed, constructed, and furnished by the local forest guard. It has two bedrooms, a dining room, one toilet, and an outhouse for a kitchen. Running water is available outside via a rubber pipe connected to a nearby stream, and beddings are also available. It is a comfortable place to rest for a couple of days, take a proper bath, wash one's clothes, and have some hot meals before beginning the return/outward journey. Next to the rest house is the *patwarkhana* (offices of the local revenue official, known as the *patwari*) and the forest guard hut. There are a total of 11 government officials in this village: the *patwari*, a forest guard, an Ayurveda compounder, a fitter from the irrigation and public health department, and seven teachers. This last category impressed us as it indicates that, in respect of education at least, the state govt has not neglected this valley. There is a primary and a middle school here with enrolments of 40 and 30 students respectively. But it is one thing to post a government employee here and quite another to ensure that he stays put. We came to know that both the fitter and the compounder had been absent for the last three weeks; the *pradhan* informed us that it was also quite common for the teachers to absent themselves for weeks at a time while showing themselves on duty! (I later discovered for myself how true this is. I was posted as education secretary of the state in 2004, and flew into Bara Bhangal sometime in September the same year in a helicopter that was going there to deliver some equipment for a micro-hydel power project. On inspecting the middle school I was shocked to find that all five teachers were on unauthorised leave for the last one month! They were all suspended and disciplinary action taken against them). This absenteeism of government officials in Bara Bhangal is a chronic problem and the higher-ups are yet to find an effective method of combating it. It happens due to the lack of any supervisory official here and the absolute confidence that no one will come from outside to check on them. There is also the perverted courage of knowing that they can't be deputed to a worse station as punishment since there is no worse station for a govt employee than Bara Bhangal! In my view, the only solution is to empower the local community through the *pradhan* of the gram panchayat—he should be authorised to mark their attendance and to sanction them leave. The political will to introduce this obvious solution, however, is lacking as the teachers are a sizeable voting block and resist being placed under a lowly *pradhan*, even if it is only for this limited purpose. So much for panchayati raj! We also discovered other oddities in government policies and practices in this valley, indicating the apathy in Shimla towards the special needs of a landlocked area like Bara Bhangal, and the lack of will to try and cater to these needs.

The main economic activities in the valley are agriculture and sheep rearing. Agriculture is basically subsistence since the cost of transporting any produce outside on mules is prohibitive: we learnt that only some rajmash (a variety of large red beans, almost a staple diet all over Himachal) is exported. The agriculture department therefore appears, very conveniently, to have given up on this valley; it has not stationed even an inspector or extension worker here. But the valley is rich in saffron and kala zeera (black cumin), which grow in the wild and are extremely high-value crops, selling for thousands of rupees a kilogramme. With a little effort these crops can be cultivated *in situ* on the farmers' fields. The flora of this area has an amazing bounty and variety, and remains untouched by any disease or chemicals. It has the potential for producing the finest honey, even organic honey. Rare and commercially valuable medicinal plants and herbs are present here in plenty, primarily because the sheer remoteness and inaccessibility of the area has meant that exploiters from outside have not been able to reach here yet. This wealth can, with a little bit of effort on the part of the forest and Ayurveda departments, be harnessed for the benefit of the local people. On the sheep rearing front, we learnt from official statistics that there are 1,47,000 head of sheep in Bara Bhangal. This, in fact, serves as the backbone of their cash economy given the absence of any agricultural surplus. The herds are migratory—in the summer months they graze on the high slopes and pastures; in the winters they migrate to the plains of Kangra, and even towards Bharmour via the Chobu Pass and Manimahesh. The shepherds sell a few heads while in the plains to meet their cash requirements. However, surprisingly enough, there are no veterinary doctors or even a pharmacist in the entire Bara Bhangal area! The shepherds are forced to fend for themselves when disease hits their herds; once every few years epidemics strike, wiping out years of laboriously accumulated capital on the hoof. The administration has not come up with any insurance schemes for the sheep either. It does dole out a niggardly few hundred rupees if a sheep dies of some disease or is killed by a wild animal, but in such cases the shepherd has to carry the carcass to Bir for a most mortem at the animal husbandry hospital there! Carrying a dead sheep on mule back to Bir would cost a thousand rupees, about twice the admissible compensation. (On our return to Shimla we took up this issue with the department and, realising the absurdity of this policy, the government has now authorised the *pradhan* of the local panchayat to issue the death certificate without a post mortem, which would be accepted by the department for purposes of providing compensation.)

There was no electricity in the village when we visited in 2003, and kerosene was also scarce since it had to be carried over the Thamsar—an expensive proposition. Cooking was done exclusively on firewood, and people used roots of the pine tree, known as *jagni*, for lighting purposes. Rich in pine oil, these stubs, about 10 inches long, are lighted and wedged on the walls. They are also carried like torches in the hand—it is an ethereal experience to see a line of lighted *jagnis* moving silently in the darkness of the night. But this was soon to change for the better: we saw a micro-hydel project under construction, financed by Himurja, the government's agency for micro power projects. (By the end of 2004 the village had been electrified: the micro-hydel scheme has been commissioned on a stream that flows past the village. It supplies power for lighting and heating to all the houses for a fixed monthly tariff of 20 rupees each. Operated by an NGO, it is nothing short of a revolution and life-changer for the residents).

We spent the night in the forest rest house, and left at 6:00 am the next morning for our return trip via Nayagram and Bharmour. The journey henceforth is entirely along the right bank of the Ravi, or, to be precise, on the right wall of the deep gorge carved out by the river. It is a two-day trek to Nayagram and one has the choice of camping for the night at any of three places en route: Khanar (18 km), Dardi (25 km), or Khurdu (32 km). We decided to carry on to Khurdu, feeling refreshed after our rest at Bara Bhangal—the hope was to cover the final eight kilometres to Nayagram quickly the next day and reach the district headquarters of Chamba by evening. But in retrospect it is advisable to camp at Dardi since the track is positively back-breaking and even dangerous. Also, covering 32 km in one day on such terrain is stretching oneself to the limits of one's endurance. Initially there is a moderate climb after Bara Bhangal, and for the first five kilometres the track is well-defined and about a metre wide: the local panchayat, with some funds received from the deputy commissioner of Kangra, has done a good job on it. At the five-kilometre point one comes to a broad nullah that has a lush green "thatch" or pasture with a stream flowing through its middle. This is Bhalaid Nullah, which forms the western boundary of Bara Bhangal and of Kangra district; from here begins the Bharmour subdivision of Chamba district. It is a good spot to have breakfast at with the sun just hitting the high peaks, and if one is lucky one can sight ghoral on the other side of the river. After Bhalaid, however, the track becomes a nightmare and makes one wish that one had returned via the Thamsar Pass. There are four successive ridges to be scaled before Khanar, each about 250–300 metres high and with a corresponding steep descent after each. The track passes through thick forests and over naked rock faces, taking one to the depths of the Ravi gorge which twists and turns like a tortured serpent. About a thousand feet above the river bed, the river is not even visible from the track at times and its roar is just a faint rumbling. There is no defined track, which is actually more like a goat track, usually not more than a foot wide. The footing is precarious and one has to literally hang on to trees, grass, and boulders to propel oneself forward. It is easier to climb than to descend since, in the latter case, one has no traction at all and a single slip could prove to be fatal. One has to be extremely careful here and take one's time; a strong, thick walking stick is invaluable for providing that extra grip and balance.

The worst stretch, even by the fearful standards described above, is just before Khanar—at this point the track simply disappears on the lip of a jutting cliff! When we reached this point, we found an old, wizened Gaddi sitting there. He strongly advised us to go back, explaining that the track ahead was fit only for goats, not even for sheep. Realising that there were a couple of government officials in our party, he then roundly cursed the authorities for doing nothing to improve the track, which actually is the only way in and out of Bara Bhangal for seven months of the year when the Thamsar is closed. However, the elderly Gaddi's choicest curses were reserved for the local MLA who, according to him, had never even visited this valley. We thoroughly empathised with him, gave him a pack of cigarettes, but decided against accepting his well-meaning advice to turn back—that was not an option any more.

Right on the edge of this cliff stands a huge tree; a big hollow has been carved out of its trunk and a statue of a goddess—Mata—placed in it. Traditionally, those making the trek from the Bara Bhangal side seek the Mata's blessings before crossing this dangerous portion, and those coming from the other side extend their gratitude to the goddess for having crossed it safely. We too prayed to the Mata and proceeded to look over the edge to see what awaited us. Below was a massive, naked rock face extending all the way down to the Ravi, about 1,500 feet below and at an impossible 90-degree sheer. It was about 100 metres wide: a 10-inch-wide ledge on the rock face served as the track for the first 25 metres, after which there was nothing except cracks and jutting rocks for the remaining 75 metres! This was the path we were supposed to take to get to the other side of the sheer rock face. The trick is not to look down and to keep moving; if one remains stationary at one place for too long, the muscles, already in spasm from sheer nervousness, tend to freeze and one becomes incapable of taking the next step. We slowly crawled along the rock wall in single file, faces and the front of our bodies pressed against the hard rock, wedging our toes into the cracks and holding on to the protuberances. Fortunately, the local *up-pradhan* and a couple of villagers had accompanied us solely to see us through this stretch, and without their help and guidance we would never have made it across. It took us about 20 minutes to negotiate this face, and our legs were trembling when we reached the other side. This rock face takes one or two lives every year. If someone slips and falls, no one even bothers to search for the body—it is pointless as the Ravi devours it, and in any case there is no way of going down. In one particularly poignant incident a few years back, we were told that a "Gaddin" lost her footing and plummeted down. Somehow she got wedged in a ledge hundreds of feet below, her body broken but still alive. There was nothing her companions could do to reach and rescue her. Therefore, rather than letting her die a lingering and prolonged death, they rolled huge rocks down on her and killed her. Nothing encapsulates the tragic loneliness and neglect of these people more effectively than this tale. After all, it would take just a few kilos of dynamite to blast a track through and across this rock face—if only the authorities cared.

The track broadens out again on the other side and descends steeply for 500 feet through thick, dry grasses. At this point the *up-pradhan* and his companions took leave of us and recrossed the rock face on their way back to Bara Bhangal! Nothing exemplifies the generosity of spirit, the depth of basic moral values, and the simple courage of these people better than this: they were happily willing to risk their lives twice in one day to help some strangers for the reason that, by the standards of their uncorrupted society, they considered it their obligation and duty! We had no words to thank these large-hearted people except the promise that we would take up their issues with the state government on our return, which we have since done with some success.

About an hour's walking later we reached Khanar, the first habitation on this route. The hamlet has 20 or so houses and a small temple. The first house is that of one Vinod Kumar, a strapping young man who works with the SSB (Sashastra Seema Bal) in Delhi. He and his pretty young wife greeted us with the warmth we were now getting accustomed to and insisted that we have tea with them. In fact, since winter was approaching, Vinod had come on leave in order to help his wife pack and move with him to Delhi. The couple own some land here, which they farm to meet their basic requirements of wheat, pulses, and rajmash. Straight in front of Vinod's house, looking southwards and across the Ravi, is a huge valley from which a stream debouches into the Ravi; at the top of the valley is Khanar Pass, an alternative route into Kangra valley. The pass itself was not visible but we could see some glaciers at the very top. Vinod Kumar informed us that he could occasionally see brown bears feeding in the valley, at the spot where it meets the Ravi, late in the evenings. We had another 14 km to cover that day, so after bidding farewell to Vinod we resumed our journey. The track improves considerably now, wider and at a gentle up-and-down gradient; it meanders through sloping fields of grass, still about 500 feet above the river. It takes two hours to reach the hamlet of Dardi, bigger and more prosperous than Khanar. The reason for this was immediately obvious—Dardi is linked by a mule track to the roadhead at Nayagram. This makes all the difference as the villagers here can send out their produce to the markets, and also bring in construction materials and other amenities to make life slightly easier. We had lunch at the house of one Shonki Ram, a prosperous farmer who also owns mules. He has a large house: double-storeyed with long running verandas, and a huge courtyard in front. We also met an extremely interesting and enterprising man by the name of Sohan Lal—an ex-postal employee, he had resigned from his cushy government job two years ago to grow apples. Now, this is not as humdrum as it sounds (!) because, even though Dardi's climate and altitude are suitable for growing apples, nobody had done so here till then due to the lack of access to the markets. However, construction of a mule track about two years ago by the authorities opened up new opportunities, which Sohan Lal wished to take advantage of and quit his job. He has now planted 450 apple plants in his lands and hopes to see them bear fruit in another four or five years. The apples from here will be the best in Chamba since the existing Bharmouri apples are grown at lesser heights and do not get the chilling which the Dardi apples will get. Moreover, the soil here is absolutely virgin and no chemicals are needed—the organic apples that these orchards will produce are bound to command a higher price in the market. Sohan Lal's initiative is nothing short of revolutionary for this region as, if successful, it can change the face of this backward region and perhaps of Bara Bhangal as a whole. And all this is being done without the dubious benefit of the hundreds of extension officers and scientists that the horticulture department pays fat salaries to! It is the initiative of an individual, not the government. Incidentally, Sohan Lal, with his postal background, had an interesting nugget of information for us: he informed us that the village of Bara Bhangal was the only revenue village in the country which did not have a postal address of its own. All letters addressed to the residents of this village are delivered in Baijnath and the addressee is supposed to make his own arrangements to have them picked up! I have not been able to verify this remarkable piece of desideratum.

We left Dardi at about 3:30 pm. The track descends sharply into a big nullah containing a frothing stream that is crossed by a wooden bridge. The trek is much easier now as the mule track is wider and the gradient gentler. It is a pleasant walk through gently sloping grasslands; the track now descends to just about 100 feet above the Ravi. After two hours one approaches Khurdu, which is not a village at all but a collection of three wood-and-stone shacks on the track in the shelter of a massive rock face, just about 20 feet above the roaring Ravi. These belong to another enterprising soul, one Milap Chand, the ex-*pradhan* of Bajol panchayat (Bajol is a big village on the way to Nayagram, about half a kilometre off the track). Milap Chand runs a reasonably good business here—his three shacks house a shop, a boarding house where about six people can tuck in for a night, and his own residence. He also keeps a few cows and sells the milk to the adjoining villages if he does not require it for his own guests. He produced a very fine dinner that

night and a bottle (not milk!) that went a long way in soothing muscles that had walked for 32 km that day!

The sixth and final day is a much easier trek in comparison, as if to make up for the previous day. All the hard climbing and clambering, and the dangerous patches had been left behind. It is eight kilometres from Khurdu to the roadhead at Nayagram over a pleasant trail that meanders through pastures for the most part. Immediately after Khurdu one negotiates a grassy mound about 250 metres in height, traversing it over 10 switchback curves along its face. On breasting the mound the track dips into grasslands, gradually descending to meet the Ravi, as if to make friends with the adversary of the last two days. To the left, across the river, one can see the 12,000-foot-high Jalsu Pass, beyond which lies Baijnath. The government has started the construction of a road over this pass to connect Nayagram and Baijnath, which shall reduce the distance between Bharmour/Holi and Baijnath by more than 100 km. This will immensely benefit the Kangra Gaddis who migrate between the Kangra valley and Bharmour twice each year. The mule track between Khurdu and Nayagram is also being realigned at a lower level to bypass the climb involved in negotiating the high grassy mound after Khurdu. There are a couple of other features which the local people will point out to you with a muted air of importance: straight ahead in the far distance to the north, one can see the dim outlines of a peak in Lahaul district, locally known as Sikandar peak. Named after Alexander the Great, local lore has it that Alexander had come as far as this peak in his quest to invade India. (This is the second reference to Alexander the Great that I have come across on my treks in Himachal. The other one is about the natives of Malana village in Kullu district, beyond the Chandrakhani Pass, being descendants of Alexander's soldiers. Neither of the two references, I believe, has been scientifically documented or authenticated). The second interesting feature here is a huge rock one crosses about five kilometres from Khurdu, perched on the slopes above the Ravi. According to the local villagers accompanying us this rock is soaked in blood for in the partition riots of 1947 a large number of Muslims were butchered on this rock! We stopped and gazed in awe at this geological specimen, not wanting to believe that the murderous passions of politics and civilisation could penetrate so far into the bosom of nature.

We reached Sadarsu three hours after leaving Khurdu, and crossed over to the left bank of the Ravi over an iron bridge that had been built a few years earlier. A small temple sits next to its right abutment and there's a poignant story attached to this temple too. When the bridge was being built a young girl fell off its incomplete structure and drowned in the river. Accepting it as just another casualty in these harsh conditions, work carried on and the bridge was finally completed. The night before it was to be thrown open, the water level in the river rose unusually, huge tree trunks carried by the torrential flood waters smashed into the bridge and destroyed its pilings. Work on rebuilding the bridge commenced but each time it neared completion, some accident or the other kept occurring. Finally, the authorities consulted a local holy man who was of the opinion that the spirit of the young girl, who had died there earlier in the accident, was haunting the site, and would never let the bridge be completed unless it was propitiated and shown due reverence. So the little temple was built in her memory and the bridge was completed. Miraculously, there were no more accidents! Local villagers come to pray at the temple of this young girl even now, grateful that she allowed their villages to be connected to the roadhead. It is little stories and myths like these that make travelling in the remotest regions such a rewarding and soul-awakening experience!

Thirty minutes of a gentle climb through thick, cool forests of pine brings one to the fairly large village of Nayagram, the servicing point for the upstream villages in the Ravi valley all the way to Bara Bhangal. It is connected by road to Holi (12 km) and the sub-divisional headquarters of Bharmour (35 km), and finally to the district headquarters of Chamba (87 km). Nayagram is serviced by two daily buses of the state road transport corporation and, as can easily be imagined, the drivers of these buses are perhaps the most important persons here! So much so that the ultimate ambition of every school kid here was to become a bus driver! We hopped on a bus to Holi—a small town

rather than a village with a school, a helipad, some government offices, a micro-hydel project, a fishery, etc. It has two very well appointed and furnished rest houses of the PWD and the forest department. Getting accommodation in them is not usually a problem, but it is still advisable to make advance reservations in case a local minister is loose in the valley, as happened with us! Cellular phone connection, though not yet available in this remote valley, should not take long to arrive. The ubiquitous public telephone (PCO), however, is very much in presence in the market of Holi and we went there to inform our families that we had made it back safely. In the PCO our connections were made by a gum-chewing young girl in jeans, and we knew then that we had arrived back in civilisation after a thoroughly satisfying, extremely demanding, and occasionally dangerous trek!

2003

Acknowledgements

$\mathcal{I}$ have been trekking the scenic and captivating mountains and vales of Himachal Pradesh for the last twenty years with a small group of close friends. Our common love for Nature and respect for the simple values it offers has proven to be a strong bond, holding our group together through all these years. They all anticipated that I would write about our shared experiences some day and constantly encouraged me in this direction; they have also provided, collectively and individually, many valuable inputs for a better understanding of natural phenomena, local communities and customs, and the impacts of developmental activities on the environment. My heartfelt thanks, therefore, to Sashi Bhai, Payson Stevens, Vinod Tewari, Kunal Satyarthi, Ankit Sood, Vineet Kumar, Harsh Mitter, Ajay Srivastava, T.D. Negi, and Inderpal.

I am particularly indebted to Sanjeeva Pandey for his many perceptive insights into the management of the Great Himalayan National Park, whose director he was for many years. His critical contribution in getting the park recognised as a World Heritage Site by UNESCO in July 2014 will always remain his crowning achievement as a forester. This had always been our dream and we can now hang up our boots with a sense of satisfaction. I know of no one else who has trekked so extensively in the GHNP and documented it so meticulously. I am also grateful to him for allowing me to use some of his photographs in this book.

My thanks to the youthful editor Siddhartha Banerjee whose suggestions have hugely improved the text. He spent many hours verifying place names, natural features, even local terms, and this has

only added to the authenticity of what is contained herein. In particular, I am indebted to him for bearing with my limited knowledge of editing software, which made his job just that much more difficult!

Many thanks are due to my son Saurabh who assisted me through the digital nightmare of formatting, downloading, proofreading, and editing, and for explaining the arcane tools that go into writing a book these days. The trekking itself was the easy part!

I am deeply indebted to Mr and Mrs Niyogi of Niyogi Books for encouraging me to publish this book, and for sparing no effort to make it attractive and presentable to the reader. In publishing this book on a niche subject they have consciously decided to veer off the beaten track, as it were, and deserve the gratitude of all nature lovers.

And finally, I cannot end without expressing my appreciation for the dedicated lower-level staff of the Himachal Forest Department— the Range Officers, Block Officers and Forest Guards. Much of the natural features described in this book would not exist today but for their efforts. I myself am neither a forester nor a local Himachali, and, therefore, whatever mountain lore and observations of wildlife I have recorded in these pages, have been gleaned by spending countless hours in their company. Their unseen contribution to this book is enormous and deserves to be acknowledged. They are performing a magnificent job in very difficult circumstances where both the official and political will to protect the natural environment is completely lacking. If the glorious natural landscapes of the GHNP survives for the next generation, we can only silently thank these unsung heroes.

Index

About the Author

Avay Shukla belongs to the Indian Administrative Service and has served in Himachal Pradesh for 30 years. He is president of the Himachal Pradesh Trekking Association, and a founder member of the Ecotourism Society of India. He is an unapologetic conservationist and has quite often found this clashing with his role as a government servant, a trait portrayed honestly in this book. His passion for nature has seen him tramping up and down the remotest areas of this mountain state for the last 20 years. His detailed account of some of the major and more difficult treks is unique in that he brings to bear on these journeys his administrative insights and experience, which adds depth and perspective to his observations and narrative.

The author is now retired and settled in a small village (pop. 225; 224 when his wife dumps him for Delhi, which is quite often) 20 km above Shimla. He is a relentless blogger and spends his remaining time tending to his apple plants and looking for golf balls that he unerringly drives into the forests every time.